Money Laundering Prevention

Deterring, Detecting, and Resolving Financial Fraud

JONATHAN E. TURNER

WILEY

John Wiley & Sons, Inc.

Published by John Wiley & Sons, Inc., Hoboken, New Jersey.

Published simultaneously in Canada.

For general information on our other products and services or for technical support, please contact our Customer Care Department within the United States at (800) 762-2974, outside the United States at (317) 572-3993, or fax (317) 572-4002.

Wiley also publishes its books in a variety of electronic formats. Some content that appears in print may not be available in electronic books. For more information about Wiley products, visit our web site at www.wiley.com.

Library of Congress Cataloging-in-Publication Data

Turner, Jonathan E., 1969-
  Money laundering prevention : deterring, detecting, and resolving financial fraud / Jonathan Turner.
        p. cm.
  Includes index.
    ISBN 978-0-470-87475-2 (hardback); ISBN 978-1-1180-8668-1 (ebk);
ISBN 978-1-1180-8669-8 (ebk); ISBN 978-1-1180-8675-9 (ebk)
  1. Money laundering—Prevention.   I. Title.
  HV6768.T88 2011
  658.4'73—dc22

                                                                    2011007525

Printed in the United States of America.

10 9 8 7 6 5 4 3 2 1

This book is dedicated to
Kristen, Sarah, and Alex,
in appreciation of their love,
support, encouragement, and
for making everything possible.

Contents

Preface

I have always been fascinated by money laundering, particularly its relationship to fraud. While the topic has long been considered the financial twin of narcotics investigations, the lack of broader interest in money laundering on its own never made sense to me. From my perspective, money laundering is the epitome of fraud methodology. It involves the concealed transfer of assets by masking them in the mundane normalcy of financial transactions. In short, the methodology of money laundering exists in every fraud scheme. As a practitioner in the field, it seemed only natural that the evolving anti-money-laundering (AML) tools would be widely recognized and used by fraud investigators and forensic accountants.

Yet nothing could be further from the truth. When I began looking and applying money laundering tests to typical fraud cases, I was often met with confusion. When I suggested that finding the individual benefit could be reversed to find the underlying fraud, I found skepticism. When I used the phrase "money laundering," I would get "But this is not a drug case" in reply.

In 2005, the Association of Certified Fraud Examiners (ACFE) approached me about updating their money laundering course and I leaped at the opportunity. It gave me the chance to reshape the conversation away from narcotics trafficking and toward white collar crime. This shift in perspective was possible, too, given the Patriot Act, which had already pushed AML compliance in the same direction with its emphasis on identifying terror financing. Since that time, I have taught this view of money laundering and its relationship to fraud dozens of times around the world. I have found audiences receptive to the idea that traditional AML tools can be applied, successfully, in white collar crime matters, even when there is no nexus to narcotics trafficking or terror financing. Similarly, the use of anti-fraud tools generates useful results in uncovering and resolving money laundering cases.

Since taking an active role in AML training in late 2005, I have continued to investigate the relationship between fraud and money laundering. In the process, I have become increasingly convinced that the distinctions are superficial and often the result of training perspectives. I have written, lectured, and researched these two dynamically growing fields, finding that the evolving tools for each have direct application to the other.

As fate would have it, I was working on a money laundering case that was structured like a traditional fraud case when Sheck Cho, my editor at John Wiley & Sons, called to see if I was interested in putting my ideas into a book. Soon after, this project was off and running.

As you read the end result—this book—consider where and how these methodologies fit other aspects of your work. If you are a regulator or investigator, an academic or practitioner, you will soon realize that the processes, procedures, and intent of money laundering apply to a much wider range of issues. You will soon be asking yourself why, if these methodologies are so well known, are they still so successful? What is it about money laundering that makes it appeal to such a diverse audience? The assumption that money laundering practices are restricted to drug dealers is not going to stand—and we know what happens when you assume in matters of fraud.

This book endeavors to put money laundering into a modern context. Rather than focusing on accounting transactions or banking regulations, the approach is to discuss the evolving incentives to launder money, the adapting technologies that help hide the movement of funds, and the huge financial gains that can be obtained by providing laundering services.

Beginning with a discussion of the money laundering process, including what it means and how it came about, I seek to explore the inherent challenges between governments and financial institutions. This provides a foundation and context to see the opportunities in any financial institution, or nonfinancial business that provides similar services.

From there, the motivations of individual participants become vital because any defense is only effective if one understands the opposing perspective and intent. Otherwise, despite effort and good intentions, defensive efforts will fail. The challenge in money laundering cases is that the methodologies appeal to a wide range of people, from criminals, such as drug dealers and embezzlers, to political individuals, like terrorists and tax protesters, to ordinary people confronted by greed. Understanding who these people are, what motivates them to cross the line, and how many ways they can become involved gives the interested investigators, regulators, and AML professionals needed insight.

Various illicit drugs are sometimes referred to as "gateway drugs" in that they lead to further and harder drug use—the reward, so to speak. In much the same way, various petty actions can be considered "gateways" to full-blown and creative methods of money laundering that reward the criminal with more liquid assets. The range of available money movement mechanisms is extensive. They do not lend themselves to simple or straightforward controls. And once an individual has successfully moved money through the system, greed can become a powerful force for further and further involvement.

Part of the challenge in investigating money laundering is the international component because all money laundering is an attempt to avoid government rule, regulation, and, very often, taxes. The use of various kinds of *entities* around the globe provides both protection from discovery and barriers to seizure of the laundered funds. But distance alone is not the driving factor. Differences in government policies and implementation leave gaps, gaps that in some cases are intentionally created because some governments benefit from illicit funds passing through or remaining within their borders. Just as individuals have their motivations, so do governments. While global AML agreements are strengthening, their impact on reducing the actual level of money laundering appears negligible. Thus, despite the growing international consensus that money laundering is a widespread and harmful criminal activity that affects all nations, certain countries continue to see practices and policies that not only allow money laundering, but they actually encourage and enable it.

Technology is impacting this process as well. Like every other aspect of modern life, technology is providing tools that change how funds flow through the financial system. Fifty years ago the primary financial tool was cash, and every country issued and operated on its own currency. If the European Union (EU) model is the future, then we can expect other economic unions, where countries embrace one currency, such as the euro, or simply adopt another country's currency, such as the U.S. dollar, or peg their own to it. Another change that has taken place in the past half century is what is meant by a "financial institution." Many variations have arisen, as banks cease to be the only choice for moving money. More choices can be found to move money, including purely virtual entities that exist entirely online. Indeed, money laundering, once virtually limited to the use of cash, has adapted along the way and has increased exponentially as the financial world went from checks to credit cards to electronic transfers—which has nearly eliminated the use of cash in general commerce. (Illicit goods are the last bastion of criminal cash transactions.)

So, as opportunity increases, a corresponding pressure is placed on the discovery and prevention aspects. An increasing series of regulations, initiatives, and legal structures have been created to provide tools to stop the free flow of funds through banking institutions. Sometimes these regulations are counter-intuitive for financial institutions because their underlying purpose is to facilitate the free flow of funds. Yet as the penalties for compliance failures increase, these institutions are being forced to find what is hidden and prevent future access by criminals. Since nobody expects money laundering to go away, this has created a competitive atmosphere where financial institutions seek to balance their regulatory requirements against their economic best interest while ensuring that their AML programs are, at least, as good as their peers.

The real pressure to make progress against money laundering came after September 11, 2001, when the connection between terror financing and money laundering methodologies was clearly demonstrated to the world. Prior to that, the link was known but not popularly understood. This shift in focus motivated many countries to increase their regulatory framework and enhance the cooperation in tracing illicit payments. Terror financing, while it uses money laundering methods, has a significant difference from white collar crimes and the like—the amounts involved can be much smaller. Where prior AML attention was focused on very large money movements, the emphasis on terror financing requires tools, techniques, and approaches that identify substantially smaller money flows.

This drove AML efforts in a new direction, an intensive look at the policies and procedures that would be required to identify potential risk areas and find exploitable opportunities before either criminals or terrorists would be able use them. The primary result was to push AML responsibilities even further out. What was once a governmental function had, over time, been given over to banks and, eventually, other financial institutions.

This risk-based approach has even pushed these responsibilities further on, to the various service providers most likely to be involved in potential laundering transactions. Interestingly, Europe has been the leader in recruiting these other players in the AML process; whereas the United States, the principal driver of most AML efforts, has lagged behind in this innovation.

Understanding that nothing can eliminate the risk, there will always be a need to investigate allegations of improper money movements. Traditionally, this has been a government role, but this responsibility, too, as with the risk policies, has shifted to the private sector steadily over the past 40 years. Much as technology has expanded the definition of a financial institution practically if not legally, the number of organizations now involved in money laundering investigations is growing. Today, launderers attempt to move money through banks, brokerage houses, insurance companies, charities, multinational service companies, and manufacturers—indeed, every kind of organization imaginable. AML is no longer merely a bank security concern. Any professional who deals with financial transactions must now be aware of—and be ready to become involved in—money laundering investigations.

The process ends with the reporting and recovery aspects. Efforts to control money laundering involve a tremendous volume of data aggregation. Where discovered, identified, or even suspected, financial institutions and related entities are required to document and report these activities. The intent is to gather sufficient data so that even if a laundering transaction succeeds, the pattern can be used to stop or intercept the next transaction. The recovery process is focused on making laundering too expensive. By seizing identified illicit funds, governments not only fund their AML efforts, they drive up the cost of this criminal conduct.

By discussing the motivations, objectives, and outcomes, I hope to present you with ideas to consider and practical information you can use. These will be tools to increase the breadth and depth of your own toolkit and enable you to bring more value to the table for your organization. This is why I wrote the book. Please consider the ideas that I present to you. See how they can be implemented in your practice. That said, I would love to know your experiences integrating AML concepts into wider fraud investigations, and how you think anti-fraud concepts can further our work in the AML field. Perhaps what you find out—and what I do—will be the next book. I can be reached at www.linkein.com/jonathaneturner.

Acknowledgments

There is no way to adequately thank all of the people who played a role in the creation of this book because nearly every person I have worked with over my career has been a part of its creation. All of my classmates and students, professors and colleagues, peers and friends, and even the perpetrators I have met through my work—each experience has helped shape me, my career, and this book.

There are some people and organizations that deserve special note. I would like to begin by thanking my business partner, Andy Wilson, for his support, humor, and occasional abuse over the 20 years we have worked together. He is an outstanding fraud investigator, a great business partner, and a true friend.

Next, I must recognize Joe Wells, Jim Ratley, and the entire staff of the Association of Certified Fraud Examiners for their unwavering support of our field. I thank them for allowing me to give back some small portion of what I have received from them in the way they have shaped my profession and for everything they have taught me.

I would like to thank the faculty, staff, and students at the Kenan-Flagler School of Business of the University of North Carolina–Chapel Hill and the Department of Criminology and Criminal Justice at the University of Memphis. The interactions with my colleagues on the faculty, the support of the staff, and the interest of students make working with them both an opportunity to teach and to learn.

I extend my deep appreciation to my clients for allowing me to work with you and your organizations during difficult and highly stressful times.

I would also like to extend my gratitude to Sheck Cho and the entire team at John Wiley & Sons for the patience they have shown with a first book, especially given the constant challenge of my practice, which extended the length of this project. They had faith in me and the book and saw it through to completion.

The following individuals also have my thanks for their assistance during specific times in my professional development: Keith Casey, Sterl Greenhalgh, Pamela Segers, Ralph Anderson, Tommy Barlow, Christi Ellaby, Bill Price, John Shearer, Jerry Harris, Annie Boucher, William Lenahan, Scott Perkins, Meike Olin, Nancy Pasternak, Jean-François Legault, Allan Bachman, Alton Sizemore, Jr., Gerry Zack, Dennis Dycus, Ed Bradbury, Bruce Dean, Joe Dervaes, James Whitaker, Richard Woodford, Martha McVeigh, Peter Callaway, Delena Spann, Bert Lacativo, Robert Blair, Joseph Ford, and Cynthia Cooper.

Finally, and, most important, I must thank my family: my parents and grandparents for making me the person I am, my wife for helping me become the person I want to be, and my children Sarah and Alex for being who they are.

CHAPTER 1

Understanding the Process of Money Laundering

What Is Money Laundering?

People often see *money laundering* as an exotic process, an objective whose very name evokes some mysterious and nefarious financial crime. In reality, it is one of the most common—and commonly misunderstood—financial activities connected to illicit financial schemes, including fraud, tax evasion, narcotics, human smuggling, corporate fraud, government corruption, and terror financing. The beauty and danger of money laundering is that it touches them all.

Anti-fraud professionals, criminal investigators, tax auditors, government prosecutors, and corporate compliance professionals are all focused on different aspects of these actions, oftentimes missing the larger picture due to an incomplete understanding of what money laundering is, how it works, and who is involved. It is important to understand the meaning, role, and history of this kind of activity to see how it began and evolved to impact a wide range of business functions. Today money laundering is a criminal business, with the emphasis on the business aspect. To merely look at one statute or another, or focus on the criminal elements involved, significantly misses the point. Today the attraction to money laundering is profit—it is a service-oriented business where readily available knowledge can position people to make significant profits with little perceived risk.

This chapter explores the origins and evolution of money laundering, tracing it to the current day, providing the foundation necessary to deter, detect, and document money laundering activities. With this foundation, the role and responsibilities of the money launderer can be explored as well as what makes money laundering so attractive to all kinds of people engaged in criminal activity. Understanding why something is done, as well as how it is accomplished, often provides the best path for defending against it. Simply calling something a "crime" is unlikely to make much of an impact where the financial benefits are often compelling.

Money Laundering Defined

What we now refer to as "money laundering" is popularly said to originate from Mafia ownership of laundries in the United States. Gangs generating illicit cash from extortion, prostitution, gambling, and other enterprises purchased legitimate businesses through which they funneled these illicit goods. True or not, the term stuck and for people seeking to legitimize cash, the laundry analogy is popularly accepted.

The reasons date back to Al Capone. Although reputed to be one of the biggest criminal leaders of his time, he was convicted of simple tax evasion. Seeing what happened to Capone forced gangsters to be more careful with the origin, accounting, and disbursement of their funds, and although the world is no longer the cash-based economy it was in the 1930s, the lessons they learned in trying to avoid criminal prosecution are still used today.

To protect the mob bosses' money from government insight, Meyer Lansky is reputed to have developed the modern money laundering approach. He created a process whereby cash from crimes in the United States was taken to Switzerland and loaned back to entities owned or controlled by the various illegal gangs. The "loan-to-back" concept, which can obscure the real timing of the illicit funds, is still one of the more popular mechanisms for laundering cash. It allows the beneficiary to document, declare, and utilize cash while providing limited recourse for government investigators.

Money laundering has been defined in a variety of ways by a variety of sources. While the definitions used by various regulators, criminal codes, and law enforcement agencies are valid, they and others like them are mostly focused on the criminal aspects, the accounting aspects, or the illicit nature of the actions. For that reason, most are incomplete to a proper understanding of the laundering process. Traditional definitions have focused on the activities involved and are usually divided into three phases: (1) placement, (2) layering, and (3) integration, or some variation on those themes. While action oriented, these definitions also cover a lot of perfectly legitimate activities. Creating an adequate definition is challenging, since the basic roles and actions are often disputed, and the process is global where the lack of common practices and codes of conduct leave room for debate about the meaning of even the word illicit. This book uses a process similar to *zero-based budgeting* in that each step in the process is built from the ground up, creating a viable definition for the objectives and actions involved in money laundering.

You have to look no further than a criminal trial to see how diligently the standard definitions are disputed, as the prosecution attempts to corral the activities under this title and the defense argues they are merely common business activities. The problem with most standard definitions is that both the prosecution and the defense are correct. Money laundering in the criminal sense involves the use of criminal or illicit funds and assigns criminal liability to otherwise legitimate business practices. Thus the first task in defining money laundering is to recognize that it is a business function. That is, *money laundering involves the use of traditional business practices to move funds and the people who engage in this activity are doing so to make money.* The mere fact that the activity has been criminalized does not change its underlying nature.

Why Do People Launder Money?

While it is possible given some psychopathic personalities, it is exceedingly rare that anyone gets involved in money laundering because he or she wanted to commit a crime. It is far more likely that the person would get involved because the activity is profitable. Treating the topic as a crime, however, misses the business realities that impact legitimate participants and financial transactions and, eventually, the investigation into the money laundering itself.

As a business activity, money laundering can further be divided among those "self-employed," who launder funds for their own use, and "service providers," who provide a commercial service to others. Again, the mere fact that these activities may or may not be legal in the jurisdiction has little bearing on the actions themselves. Thus a more complete definition has to encompass both the personal actions and the professional initiatives.

This leads to the motivations of the actors in money laundering. If the intent is to hide illicit funds, then the transactions will have no or limited legitimate business purposes. Here there is a clearly differentiating action. Where the process serves a legitimate business function, it will take the path of least resistance. In other words, people being people do things in the simplest and most straightforward way to accomplish the task. When laundering illicit funds, however, there is no legitimate business function being served and thus the actions often violate this rule of human nature. Since the aberration is due to the laundering objective, it provides support for an actionable definition of the process.

Thus far the definition includes a business process that provides a means for profit, either on an individual or service provider basis, whereby overly complicated mechanisms are used to mask the infusion of illicit funds into legitimate commerce. But is that complete? Or is there more to understanding exactly what is being done?

To test if there is more, look at the question of the origin of the funds. Are the actions taken related to the underlying illicit nature of the funds? Surprisingly, the answer is no. Tax evaders, spouses seeking to hide parts of the marital estate, corrupt politicians, embezzling employees, and terrorists all use astoundingly similar mechanisms to hide the movement of money.

People looking to hide the movement of funds are interested in two primary things: (1) safety and (2) secrecy. They are looking for mechanisms that will allow them to move the money with minimal risk of loss and keep the knowledge of those movements hidden from perceived adversaries. This is instructive into the thinking and mechanisms chosen.

Consider the lesson of Eliot Spitzer, the former New York governor who was involved in a prostitution ring. His long career as a prosecutor and politician should have given him the knowledge necessary to hide his actions (that is, allegedly paying a prostitute) from the government entities he served. Yet, despite his knowledge of how the government investigations were conducted, his actions fell squarely within their view. Why? Look at what he was trying to do. He was focused on hiding his alleged activities from his wife—she being the perceived adversary. He was not worried about hiding his actions from law enforcement per se because he was not hiding his financial transactions from an investigation. He did not care that he was "Client no. 9"; he cared that his wife did not discover he was "Client no. 9." Thus the perceived adversary is extremely important in differentiating and defining the money launderer's actions.

When the money launderer identifies the perceived adversary, he can make all kinds of adjustments to the scheme and go undetected for years. This can be seen by looking back at the Barings Bank scandal of the 1990s. Nick Leeson, in his book *Rogue Trader* describes being caught several times over the course of his unauthorized speculative trading. He recounts how each time he was able to talk his way out of discovery because the people who caught him did not understand what he had done. So the structure of the transactions depends on who the likely discoverer could be and what they are likely to look at or for.

Another fraudster from the 1990s, Walt Pavlo, makes the same point in his published statements. He describes knowing what the auditors would look for and providing them with distractions to keep them away from what he was hiding. In other words, these overly complicated mechanisms described above are not incidental; they are required to conceal the activities from discovery.

The Money Laundering Cycle

The definition of money laundering now needs to expand to encompass a series of actions where the money launderer conceals his actions from a perceived threat—but not from all possible lines of discovery. This leads him to create façades, illusions that can only prevent scrutiny from the perpetrator's chosen direction or perspective.

Further, the actions are not only taken to hide, but they are taken to legitimize. An essential element in the process is the conversion of a wide range of illicit funds, including proceeds of street crime, narcotics trafficking, official corruption, corporate fraud, kickbacks, bribes, and even terror financing into apparently legitimate income. While a small portion of laundered funds are intended to be hidden for some period of time, the eventual purpose will be for the initiator to publicly use the funds. The mechanisms, therefore, must use otherwise legitimate types of transactions, otherwise legitimate entities, and involve otherwise legitimate intermediary purchases to create the appearance of legitimacy. This concept, *renting credibility*, is often why and how ordinary organizations are involved in money laundering transactions. And since they provide a vital service to the money launderer, they are often compensated for their roles, which is an incentive to ask limited questions or to look the other way entirely.

This ability, and often willingness, to compensate people and organizations for their involvement creates a subtle encouragement for both participation and silence. Such entities may justify their involvement as saying that they did nothing different, but since they have accepted compensation for their role, their motives are clouded by at least the appearance of potential impropriety. Even when their actions appear otherwise ordinary, the fact that they have been compensated changes their motivation. As a for-profit enterprise, money laundering operators used compensation, coercion, bribery, and other forms of illicit pressure to induce otherwise law abiding citizens to become participants in the scheme. The use of ordinary individuals further produces the appearance of legitimacy and concealment for the money laundering operation. It also serves to decrease the likelihood that when found it will appear to be a criminal enterprise. Thus the definition must be expanded to include the attraction of individuals with no criminal objectives but purely financial objectives, who will become partners and promoters of the scheme.

So this yields a definition of money laundering that encompasses a range of otherwise ordinary business activities that are designed to hide the illicit source of funds, the illicit use of funds, the control of funds, or obscure the purpose of the funds from outside parties and provide privacy, access, and legitimacy to the end-user. The process appears harmless, enticing many people to actively consider participation and, when under stress, becomes an acceptable action. This creates a shared purpose, process, and role, where otherwise ordinary individuals and hardened criminals appear to act the same way. By hiding among the sheep, the wolves are much more successful. In laundering money, people seek to disguise the source origin or destination of cash, ending with the appearance of legitimate funds. Were the underlying funds legitimate, there would be no need for the time, risk, and expense of the laundering process. So money laundering, as the term is used today, indicates illegal conduct, but can involve any inappropriate financial behavior, including violent crimes such as extortion, drug trafficking, and arms smuggling; and nonviolent crimes, such as embezzlement, fraud, and corruption; and even personal motives, such as tax evasion and divorce. While resolving money laundering transactions is often like solving a puzzle, the model revolves around three related steps:

1. Placement
2. Layering
3. Integration

The first step, placement, generates the cash. This can consist of any activity that creates cash that the recipient wants to hide. It may involve the sales of legal or illegal products, the acceptance of improper payments, or the removal of company assets. Whatever the source, the result is money, usually cash, which could implicate the individual unless its origins can be disguised. Most commonly, the money will be deposited into a financial account with a bank, investment firm, or insurance company. To further obscure the path, money may be shipped to foreign financial organizations or used to buy works of art or other high-value items such as aircraft, boats, precious metals, and jewelry. Each possible path involves its own costs and risks, so it is clear that people would not use this process if the funds were legitimate.

The second step in money laundering, layering, involves stratifying the financial transaction. Since the objective is to hide the origins, the more layers that are added to the process, the harder it will be to prove the illicit basis for the funds. This can involve shifting the funds from account to account, or moving them from institution to institution. Once the funds are in the financial system, it is quite easy to move them around the world if necessary. Depending on the complexity of the movements, and the secrecy desired, these layers can become costly. Merely moving money from account to account is inexpensive but also easy to trace. Shifting the money through various asset types incurs costs for buying and selling, but is more effective at hiding the sources. Layers often include various financial accounts, high-value items, currency and equipment sales, and the purchase of real estate and legitimate businesses, particularly in the leisure and tourism industries. Some countries are structured to assist in these transactions and legal and accounting firms in these countries often assist in setting up shell companies to help layer the transactions. In these instances, working with a local attorney, various bank secrecy laws, and attorney–client privilege, enterprising money launderers can move huge sums of money around the globe.

The final step integrates the funds in the perpetrators life. Here the illicit income is returned in a form that appears legitimate and will withstand ordinary scrutiny. This integration is often as creative as the layering process, and a certain parity should be expected here. For example, using front companies to "borrow" funds from the foreign financial institution holding the illicit funds because the "loans" are guaranteed by the deposits and the "lending" institution faces no risk. Another common approach is the over-invoicing of goods or services, again sold to either front companies or foreign institutions.

Money Laundering Is a Criminal Business

Outside of law enforcement circles, and the criminals who used the methodology, the term "money laundering" is actually relatively new. It appears to have come into the public eye during the Watergate scandal, where the methodology was used to obscure payments to criminals, and spawning the infamous "follow the money" mantra of financial investigations. One court case, *United States v. $4,255,625.39* (551 F. Supp 314 (1982)), found the term reaching acceptance throughout the U.S. judiciary.

Since then, the term has achieved common acceptance around the world. While early U.S. efforts to criminalize this pattern of international activity were cautiously reviewed, a substantial change in cooperation occurred after 2001. The clear connection between terror financing methodology and money laundering techniques ushered in a much greater level of cooperation among the world's governments.

Big business can become involved in combating money laundering. Large companies, especially financial institutions, are very attractive to money launderers, so, through regulations and evolving business practices, governments have established comprehensive anti-money-laundering (AML) systems. These systems aim to raise awareness of the place—both in government and on the part of the business—and then provide the necessary legal or regulatory devices to help resolve money laundering issues.

From a criminal investigation standpoint, the approach has been to use fines and forfeiture statutes to fund AML efforts. Law enforcement agencies find, seize, and ultimately draw their resources from the confiscation of criminal assets. Legal changes have allowed the exchange of data among public and private entities, making enforcement efforts more productive. These structural approaches have been reproduced in other countries as well.

This is extremely important in the development of the global AML programs. They model the benefits of aligning the regulatory and administrative law enforcement processes with the financial regulations, while giving consideration to the problems faced by responsible financial institutions. This requires that these institutions forgo certain types of transactions, establishing AML programs, customer identification requirements, record beneficial holders, and verify compliance with applicable regulatory requirements.

Money Laundering Is Global

So, given the renewed focus and move toward greater global integration on money laundering crimes, how is that impacting the overall process? Unfortunately, there is no evidence that money laundering is being impacted by these changes. The wide range of diverse legal and regulatory requirements means that enterprising criminals can find more opportunities to exploit these differences. Any national plan should be compatible with global standards and flexible enough to respond to new money laundering schemes.

In many countries, criminals can respond to the new regulations much faster than the authorities are able to review and revise the regulations. This means that the authorities are often forced to proceed to the financial component of the assessment in an environment that may be either too weak or legally ineffective to deal with this problem. For these reasons, governments must continue to revise their standards toward greater levels of transparency and cooperation to limit these exploitable differences.

The design of large-scale money laundering nearly always includes cross-border elements, since money laundering is a worldwide, global cooperation. The number of programs that have been established include those sponsored by international organizations such as the United Nations or the Bank for International Settlements, and at least 80 such agreements were made in the late twentieth century. Following the Financial Action Task Force, created in 1989, various governmental and cooperative entities (e.g., the European Union, the European Commission, and the Organization of American States) created regional working groups to establish AML measures based on the legal and regulatory requirement of their members. The Caribbean, Asia, Europe, and South Africa have also created regional AML task force–like organizations. Countries in West Africa and Latin America have also done the same.

Since money laundering is illegal, those criminals involved mask their transactions, blending them in with larger accounts with higher activity in the legitimate economy. This makes their individual transactions much more difficult to find. As technology has increased, it has simplified both the mechanisms for moving money and the incentive to use the global financial network for both individuals and organizations involved in crimes that involve the crime of money laundering as well.

Making use of jurisdictional differences as well as differences in laws and treaties around the globe, criminals moving money internationally present unique challenges to the investigation. The combination, too, of changing language, changing time zone, and rapidly moving money all combine to hamper recovery and regulatory enforcement. And coordination of regulatory bodies is countered by less cooperative or less observant jurisdictions, some of which facilitate money laundering.

Money Launderers Adapt Technology

This development exploits new technologies, system projects, and personnel actions, as well as other places where boundaries may be weakened to expand worldwide movement of illicit funds. The willingness to spend money to hide the origin of the funds attracts the assistance of professional intermediaries, most commonly lawyers, accountants, and bankers (every profession has its ethically challenged members), who have appeared in significant numbers to provide their services. Experts who have the ability to cover up the source of funds maintain public offices, and often times high-profile positions, creating and supporting the purported legitimacy of their methods. This comfortable existence, and the profits generated by these activities, has enabled illicit funds to gradually infiltrate the legitimate financial and economic markets.

Over time, this service industry has grown and matured, with the involved professionals assisting in the maintenance of individual criminals and expansion of corruption through their activities. Coordination of money movements with legitimate proceeds, in particular, is organized by these service providers to further limit the likelihood of discovery and recovery. These service providers use careful management of the financial balances and the changing jurisdictional rules to prevent or avoid the attention of the regulatory system—sometimes using multiple roundtrip financial transactions to reduce the possibility of detection.

As facilitators of money laundering, service providers in concert with criminals seek countries that demonstrate less respect for the global AML legislation. They use or create shelters, which are often in offshore banking centers that provide both banking services and commercial secrecy. They also supply the human face of trust, which is used to cover large-scale coordination of assets controlled by and for the benefit of the criminal money launderer. Since 1996, the International Monetary Fund (IMF) has seen a continuing increase in the flow of illicit funds coming from drugs and related money laundering, corruption, and tax evasion as compared to global economic growth. Given the pace of technological change and the ever increasing ease of complex financial movements, it is likely that an even higher share of the world's financial transactions will be used to mask the flow of illicit funds.

The Role of Technology

A growing number of Web sites to attract overseas transfers of funds, for online gambling or virtual banking, provide additional means to move money globally with limited or no restrictions. In addition, encryption technologies provide better means for hiding transactions and anonymity for those involved. All that is required is a computer. The use of technology and its impact on laundering money cannot be overstated. Technology did not create money laundering, but it did bring about a new dimension in remote destinations such as Vanuatu, Nauru, and the Marshall Islands, which might be hard to reach in person but are only a click away online.

Virtual banking, as well as online access to traditional banks, has enabled these locales to increase their financial posture, attracting capital as well as illicit funds. By layering transactions carefully through entities in these countries, money launderers are able to mask themselves and thus secure their funds in mainstream banking centers without detection.

Technology has also had an impact on the prosecution aspect. Where transactions used to be relatively slow and documentation took time to process, the pace of investigation and prosecution seemed appropriate. But the pace of transactions had increased dramatically. Today, it is possible that a defendant will learn he is a target and have time to electronically transfer funds around the globe before the legal mechanisms can be used to stop him. While some countries, such as the United States, have faster mechanisms, these are not universal. Further, most legal systems require sufficient proof before acting, and getting this level of proof requires the cooperation of the source country. Where the money is connected to political leaders or close connections, the needed law enforcement cooperation will never materialize. In many countries, only specific activities constitute a basis for money laundering, leaving the door open to safely move illicit funds through.

The Role of Banks

Simply put, what is today called money laundering was once simply called "banking." The secure handling and movement of funds is banking and, for most of history, banks were not concerned with their customers' source of funds. As regulatory environments have modernized, more and more activities have been proscribed. But this places financial institutions in a difficult place. When regulations are used to prohibit natural *and* profitable behavior, the temptation to bend and break the regulations increases. The globalization of the banking sector also means that where one bank is prohibited but another is not, the competitive pressure can also influence the choices. Offshore banks have jumped into the service environment, as affluent individuals demand confidentiality and are willing to pay for specialized services. By the end of 1997, international financial institutions held more than half of all global cross-border assets.

The exceptions to this trend have been financial institutions in the United States and Switzerland. However, the various government actions to freeze and confiscate illegal funds have been ineffective in curbing the total market for illicit funds. In the most important other financial centers, such as in the United Kingdom and Germany, there has been a huge increase in potentially suspicious transactions, yet no accompanying increase in individual criminal prosecution or confiscation of assets. Thus, while there are more regulations and more interest in terror financing and narcotics smuggling, there have been proportionally fewer financial crime arrests, indicating the relative safety of money laundering activities in these countries. More and more of these transactions occur in offshore banking centers, such as Grand Cayman, the Isle of Man, Malta, Cyprus, and other jurisdictions.

It is important to note that not all offshore banking is money laundering. Yet because of the huge growth in legitimate offshore transactions, money launderers are able to hide their transactions. Global business efforts, combined with unstable political environments, rapidly changing currency valuations, and competitive tax structures, all encourage the movement of legitimate funds along the same channels. Thus on a daily basis huge sums of money are moved around the world, providing, in essence, a river of money to hide the illicit transactions. For the most flagrant abusers, there is no economic infrastructure or meaningful regulatory process to monitor the financial transactions. In these countries, businesses are taking advantage of the bank secrecy these locales offer. Many countries in the Caribbean have established large legitimate banking services, which provide legitimate services to large enterprise customers around the world. This combination of high volumes of legitimate financial transactions with high levels of secrecy and protection become magnets for money launderers.

The Role of Nations

Money laundering is also aided by the historical strength of the U.S. dollar. Because of the devaluation of so many other currencies, there has been a strong demand for the dollar as well as other strong currencies across the globe and sometimes a correspondingly lesser inclination by countries seeking the security of stronger currencies to question the source. They become offshore havens, where capital is tax free and the emphasis is more about the collection of funds than the development of monitoring systems. Money launderers, seeking to conduct business with strong currencies, have found willing takers in developed and developing governments who have also become willing service providers in the movement and cleaning of illicit funds for mutual benefit.

One need only look at the rapid evolution of electronic financial transactions among large banks, offshore banking and financial organizations, currency exchanges, brokerage houses, gold dealers, casinos, and cash protection and processing companies to see the market that exists between money launderers and their service providers. And proficiency has become important. As with all smuggling activities, knowing what to do and how to do it correctly achieves a degree of success. Since these same activities appeal to the narcotics dealer, the corrupt politician, the employee thief, the tax evader, and so on, a large number of people have the incentive to push further developments in this area. The perception of limited risk for money laundering and, specifically, to the professionals, whether business people or government bureaucrats, who help run the processes further encourages participation from ever more otherwise law-abiding people. Many organizations have historically chosen to look away from these activities because they profit from them and/ or view them as a cost of doing business internationally. The efforts that the Organisation for Economic Co-operation and

Development (OECD) has sponsored to reduce global tolerance and to limit and restrict foreign places to hide money have not yet led to any significant reduction in the volume of funds being laundered.

When government officials take a bribe, they will often seek to expatiate it to protect the funds from discovery. Since money laundering laws rely on an underlying crime, the key to reduced attention then becomes *geographically* separating the crimes from the proceeds. For many years it was hard to get foreign governments to focus on money laundering proceeds in their jurisdictions because the perpetrators went to great lengths to ensure they did not commit any crimes in those countries. Even today, in an atmosphere of greater cooperation, unless a clear reason can be made for one country to act on the behalf of another in its attempts to counter terror financing, prosecute international criminals, and the like, enforcing another country's financial laws is often a low priority. This gray area, where cooperation doesn't exist, results in a "safe zone" where individuals can manipulate the system and remain protected, not by the legal framework but rather by the "structural" inhibitors to money laundering investigations.

Regional Hotspots

Money laundering is a growing concern in a number of Latin American countries of the MERCOSUR (*Mercado Común del Sur*, or Southern Common Market) and generating increasing challenges for regulators and law enforcement, despite improved AML tools and technology. This is partly related to the drug lords in Colombia and Mexico who need to clean their own money and larger facilities to enable them to administer the flow of funds in their own countries and regionally. In addition, it is due to foreign banks in Latin America and the Caribbean, which now includes 43 percent of the total global increase. The most visible manifestation of the money has been funneled into construction projects in tourist destinations, such as Cancun. The resulting hotel business is used to launder money. This is not limited to Mexico, as similar models have been found in other tourist areas and in luxury developments in Argentina. Stronger notification and regulations are being instituted across the Southern Common Market, focusing on potential money laundering through products, companies, and currency exchange brokers.

In Brazil, the largest economy in South America, funds from white collar crime, narcotics, and weapons smuggling are routinely laundered. Taking advantage of both regional rivalries and political differences, Brazil has become a popular banking center.

Paraguay, which is one of the most important money laundering centers in Latin America, chose to exacerbate the problem by actively pursuing banking business. By promoting policies that ensure secrecy, countries attract illicit funds. Estimates are that 20 percent of the drug-related money laundering is in Paraguay.

Until recently it has been difficult to perceive money laundering as an important issue and has resulted in the existing cumbersome means of a global legal compliance. In addition, the regulation of these areas has been resisted by financial institutions, as it is highly profitable for them. All organizations are resistant to rules that limit their profits. In this case, competing economic needs have made either covert or overt acceptance of funds, no matter the source, acceptable in many places. Money always seeks shelter, protection, and secrecy. Between dictators seeking to expatriate their stolen funds, the global narcotics trade, and the global weapons trade, there has been an ever-expanding interest in safe and secure financial transactions. This is met by increasing governmental regulation and technology for tracing transactions, resulting in ever increasingly complex money movement mechanisms.

As an example, with the end of the Cold War, large sums of money began flowing in and out of former Soviet bloc countries. Due to political instability, many business transactions are conducted through offshore business centers. These huge money flows masked the rise and impact of organized crime in these countries, allowing them the ability to launder money through the most important economic centers and offshore locations. The new focus on corruption and its impact on the money laundering process is an attempt to reverse this trend.

The Birth of the Financial Action Task Force (FATF)

In 1989, the Financial Action Task Force (FATF) was established at the G-7 Summit in Paris to develop and aid in the implementation of AML policies and practices on a national and international level and to coordinate solutions and make money laundering more difficult. The following year the FATF 40 Recommendations provided a framework that was subsequently amended in 1996. FATF grew to include 36 members and helped to set global standards for processes, procedures, regulation, and monitoring of money laundering activities. The first efforts were aimed at setting standard legal definitions and urging countries to adopt more uniform legal regulations. While this was generally successful, there are still wide differences in the underlying crimes for the basis for money laundering. Laws against narcotics trafficking are nearly universal. But other crimes such as human trafficking, tax evasion, official corruption, and white collar crime are treated differently in regard to the money laundering statures of different countries. The FATF provides guidelines for a consistent global model, but its implementation is not uniform and this allows money launderers to still take advantage of variations in different countries' legal frameworks.

By creating coordinated processes and definitions, even with some differentiation, the objective of the FATF is to enhance the effectiveness and efficiency of global AML efforts. This includes the confiscation of identified illicit funds, the identity of account holders, the retention of records, and the creation of reporting procedures, all tools for tracking financial transactions through the global financial community.

Financial institutions are required to monitor and report large and suspicious transactions—albeit this does not imply that competent authorities will investigate or track suspicious transactions to final recipients. These guidelines further extend to all financial products, including personal and business banking, private banking, and investments. (Similar guidelines apply to insurance companies.) These guidelines extend beyond the named account holder to reasonable beneficiaries' known associates (as is characteristic of business and criminal—enterprises). They also encourage regulators to take a close look at laws to provide appropriate mechanisms for international cooperation regarding suspicious transactions and in confiscation, mutual assistance, and extradition.

FATF issues annual reports on compliance, effectiveness, and recommended enhancements. Over time, these reports have helped encourage countries to adopt many of the FATF guidelines. As of late 2010, there were only two counties listed as not being in compliance—Iran and North Korea. However, there were 31 countries with significant deficiencies. Analysis of these countries indicates that money laundering has a strong financial impact. Were the benefits of allowing these activities not in their interests, these countries would more fully implement AML policies. Since money laundering can be highly profitable, however, these countries permit it and there is considerable pressure against any real compliance.

Agreement is, nevertheless, continuing to increase in the development of AML policies in many countries. This agreement is related, in large part, to the degree that money laundering activities impact their financial situation. This is largely a diplomatic effort to enhance the regulatory processes because the past practices have proven ineffective. Now the focus is not legitimate tax avoidance, but the cost and impact of international criminal activity, terror financing, the risk of official corruption, and, most recently, the impact on national economies. As an aggregate, it is the scale of illicit financial transactions that seems to have motivated countries to view the risks more seriously.

Conclusion

By using overseas accounts, individuals and business entities seek to protect themselves from the volatility of banking institutions while protecting their ability to access the funds anywhere in the world. Unfortunately, this same process works to help corrupt persons and entities avoid legal authorities and secure their ill-gotten gains. The primary challenge of money laundering is that its activities often appear perfectly normal, unless one knows the illicit origins of the funds. This is why money laundering is so successful.

AML efforts such as FATF require the coordination of all financial institutions and regulators across national borders to identify the origin and recipients of financial transactions. As these efforts improve, the perpetrators work to add layers, making compliance ever more difficult to achieve. Between economic priorities and technology, the race to keep up can outpace the capabilities of many countries willing to combat money laundering.

CHAPTER 2

Motivations for Getting Involved

Involvement Is Personal

The appeal of money laundering activities is far and wide. Though the traditional perspective is that these activities are limited to the criminal class, the reality is the participants' motivations are as varied as the mechanisms of the schemes themselves. Frankly, the problem is so widespread because the perception is that it is so limited—as long as people are not looking, participants can flourish.

As defined in Chapter 1, the activities that comprise money laundering, while possibly illegal in a given jurisdiction, are business-based activities. They are intended to make the participants money and provide a real return on investment. Thus these activities appeal to both participants seeking to move money undetected and providers seeking to profit from the service.

The participants include the traditional drug dealers and other established criminals who are reluctant to submit to the scrutiny required in modern banking relationships. They are also domestic and commercial litigants seeking to hide assets, tax-averse persons and businesses, corrupt public and private officials seeking to conceal ill-gotten gains, and the like. Each comprises a different class of people who take different paths to the same solution—to move money in secret—and this makes the money laundering process appealing.

These participants have the choice of developing their own laundering program or using a "commercial" money laundering service. The Internet can be searched to find specific instructions for the self-sufficient money launderer, including instruction videos, blog postings, and step-by-step instructions.

As commerce moves away from traditional paper currency and coin cash-based exchanges to the various forms of digital currency, money laundering is poised to become a highly viable and increasingly profitable business. Its expansion across the banking, finance, and corporate networks of today is hampered by cash-based controls. Even despite the challenges of moving large amounts of cash, money launderers have found ever more creative ways of evading detection. As technology transitions people from cash to digital currencies, these cash-based controls and protections will fade from viability, increasing the potential profit from these schemes.

People Weigh the Odds of Success

This is the proverbial cat-and-mouse game that has always existed—we try to protect something; they try to overcome the defenses. As time and technology move forward, we have a tendency to relax our guard, assured by the protections of old; while the money launderers have the motivation to innovate, inspired by the benefits they gain from success.

Since money laundering, by practical definition, is the art of moving money without attracting notice, the influx of digital transactions provides a much larger dataset within which these transactions exist. Furthermore, since they are no longer limited to a small number of very large transactions, but can rely on automated technology to spread a much larger number of correspondingly smaller transactions, the perceived safety of this fraud style is actually increasing. This is the prime motivator for potentially involved parties—the perceived risk is low, the perceived gains are high, and the pace of technological change creates an air of opportunity not seen in the United States since the gold rush of the 1800s.

Individual motivation can then be summed up as the quest for personal profit. But this profit can and does take a range of forms. It can range from the free use of ill-gotten funds, proceeds from crime, corruption, embezzlement, and other traditional criminal acts to tax evasion, avoidance of personal judgments and financial commitments, and even conducting business that is not allowed under various national or international laws.

As discussed thus far, technology has revolutionized many aspects of modern life, with the products, processes, and business practices quickly following. Modern AML controls are overwhelmingly focused on the cash conversion process, seeking to identify and highlight the movement of large amounts of cash. These controls intend to identify and isolate potentially irregular activity for further review, thereby detecting money laundering. But just as file sharing and person-to-person technologies overwhelmed the music industry, peer-to-peer payment methodologies are making the most common AML controls appear more and more like the Maginot Line—theoretically impressive, but inadequate to the task.

Within this context, the appeal to become involved in these schemes becomes more obvious. The appeal to traditional criminals, narcotics traffickers, and corrupt politicians is obvious—but what of the common man? Persons convicted of money laundering have many motivations, most common among them is the illegal narcotics trade, followed by tax evasion, creditor evasion, other criminal acts, and even terror financing. Thus the universe of potentially involved parties includes nearly any financial customer. Nearly any customer can be potentially involved in money laundering transactions, and protecting the organization is not about screening out known criminals; it is about recognizing the business imperatives that drive human actions.

Where Do Laundered Funds Come From?

It is easy to understand why the narcotics trafficker and the terrorist launder money—it is a required part of their illegal process. But it is just as important, even more so, to recognize the appeal that money laundering has to lawyers, accountants, doctors, and other ordinary people who get involved because of the real or perceived financial issues in their lives.

Where do illicit funds come from? Here's a list:

- Diversion of legitimate proceeds
- Embezzlement from employer
- Schemes to defraud others
- Tax evasion
- Personal asset protection
- Undocumented income
- Illegal acts

Hiding these funds creates a market—and attracts the service providers who facilitate money laundering.

Money laundering is notoriously hard to measure and a metric that can put a figure on the undetected transactions is elusive. But the figure most often cited is 2 to 5 percent of the global domestic product ($882,889,000,000 to $2,207,223,000,000 in 2006). This represents a significant motivation for both individuals and service providers.

Clearly this makes the industry financially viable for both the participants and the service/support entities (including governments) that profit from it. Most of the funds laundered come from the developed nations, as that is where most of the funds are, and also where some of the highest effective tax rates are found. Money, or more specifically greed, is the underlying driver that motivates people to engage in money laundering activities. Legally obtained funds may be subject to tax, so hiding funds to reduce tax exposure can motivate people. Illegally obtained funds are also subject to tax, but they are also proof of wrongdoing and a much greater motivation for people to engage in money laundering. Money laundering is therefore popular with people who have both legal and illegal sources of income and, when combined with the perception of low risk, results in corresponding low barriers to individual involvement. Lately these same mechanisms have been seen in terror financing, divorce, fraud matters, and other litigation, indicating an expansion of the areas where people believe that they can keep or use these funds without government oversight.

Large-scale money laundering involves the profits from illicit acts, tax evasion, fraud, and corruption. But it also includes the myriad individuals who are seeking to launder smaller sums. From the drug kingpin to the low-level embezzler, the underlying objective is the same: Protect their ill gotten gains from the sight and reach of government authorities.

The Impact of Corruption

When it comes to bribery and corruption, there are no international borders—just more complex problems. Bribery and corruption are age-old techniques for influencing people and decisions. Their historical roots reach back to before recorded time, and society has been struggling to limit their effect for just as long. Typically, bribery and corruption are seen as abuses of government officials or processes. But their effects reach into even the most private dealings of companies and organizations worldwide.

This section focuses on the corrosive impact that cash can have on both organizations and individuals rather than on its illegality and the specific laws being violated. Globalization in commerce has created enhanced opportunities for all types of businesses, including criminal businesses such as money laundering. Alongside that growth has been an expansion of official and government services. Together, they have created an abundance of opportunities for unscrupulous individuals with a wide range of motivations. These risks can generally be separated into three categories:

1. Criminal enterprise schemes.
2. Schemes specific to individual locations.
3. Insider or employee schemes that take advantage of the holes in the control processes, as well as exposures brought on by the organization's (voluntary or involuntary) involvement in these schemes.

There are a growing number of cases that have arisen from the combination of increased acceptance of international business practices and continued ignorance of the cultural and legal differences between countries. This is compounded by the spectacular growth in the investment arena. Together, these factors have produced an explosion in international business arrangements.

Why Is Corruption Increasing?

The most common area involves the simple globalization of business itself. Established control processes do not translate well to the variety of legal and cultural systems that permeate the international community. Thus, an organization, whether it has numerous international locations or even one key foreign trading partner, has opportunities for failure in the control process.

Similarly, the increased number of foreign vendors and supply outlets, as well as cutthroat competition in some areas, has increased the pressure on these potential failure points. The nature of the world's various tax codes has also contributed to the problem by encouraging individuals and companies to create complex structures to avoid taxes, rather than straightforward and more transparent arrangements. These elements combine to make it more difficult to police worldwide operations effectively.

These issues almost guarantee that every person involved in international business or representing their country abroad will encounter bribery and corruption on a regular basis. And how specifically they are dealt with is important, as failing to take the matter seriously can create another area of exposure to money laundering. For companies with a U.S. presence, there are two specific pieces of relevant legislation. The first is the Federal Corporate Sentencing Guidelines, spelling out the range of criminal sanctions for businesses that violate federal law. The second is the Foreign Corrupt Practices Act, which can place severe penalties on companies found to have been involved in corruption or bribery of foreign public officials.

Since many money laundering schemes involve corruption at some level, simply being a participant in a scheme can create an exposure under these laws. Understanding the extent of the vulnerabilities provides the foundation for the investigation of international bribery and corruption cases. The elements that make this type of scheme successful also illustrate the key vulnerabilities and weaknesses that must be explored for a thorough investigation of the allegation of either official or commercial corruption.

29

Corruption Always Begins Small

The first foundation piece comes from an old political acronym: NIMBY, that is, Not In My Back Yard. This term is commonly thrown about when the populace is calling for additional high-security prisons, which, of course, nobody wants built in their town. However, in dealing with international corruption cases, every country, culture, and region has certain indigenous attributes that are different from place to place. Many cultures simply do not regard some level of corruption as wrong, and for decades money laundering fell into this category. Consider the implications of the following example.

An international businessman arrived in a foreign country and presented his passport at the immigration desk. The clerk flipped through and noted the large number of entry and exits stamps from around the world. He whistled a couple of times and then told the arriving businessman, "Big problems with your visa." Unsure what to do, the businessman waited. The clerk repeated, "Big problems with your visa—it will take a lot of time to fix." At this point, a coworker, who was traveling with this businessman, reached out and provided the clerk with a $20 bill, which promptly resolved the "big problem." Meeting with government officials the next day, the businessman was assured that the country was an excellent place to do business, as the current administration had eliminated corruption. From their perspective, this was not corruption because all travelers were being treated equally.

The next key is recognition of the economic realities of the countries involved. For many citizens of developed nations, traveling to developing nations exposes them to a tremendous range of economic realities.

For sales and marketing personnel, as well as operations managers and even law enforcement personnel, the dramatic increase in economic clout can lead them to make serious mistakes. In the example above, a business traveler casually bribed the immigration officer, even though in many countries this kind of transaction is a "gratuity," like a tip. Exposure to that type of petty graft can inure the person to the realities of the situation and make that person much more willing to get involved in more serious issues.

The final key is recognition that people are human. They make mistakes, they respond differently under pressure, and they react in accordance with their background, culture, and traditions.

To successfully mitigate instances of possible bribery and corruption involving employees, vendors, and business partners on a global basis, organizations must be prepared to adjust their perceptions of these three focus areas.

Bribery and Corruption of Your Employees

All organizations, including law enforcement and other government agencies, must be constantly vigilant that their own employees are not compromised because they are the most visible line of defense against money laundering. The unfortunate reality is that a disturbing percentage of the population will advance their own agenda, through theft, embezzlement, abuse of trust, espionage, or other means if given the chance. And corrupt employees eliminate the value of good AML policies and procedures. All internal controls, including AML procedures, are designed to deter and detect wrongdoing but they depend on the integrity of the employees to be effective. As such, organizations design and implement a control process to limit the employees' ability to be compromised. Since all that these processes can do is set limits, organizations will still have allegations that require investigation.

When placed far from home, in a country that can have a different culture, mores, language, and so on, employees will be under additional stress. They will be exposed to a wide range of new influences, both positive and negative, and they will be without the comfortable influences of home. In this environment, they may be more susceptible to approaches from either tempted individuals or outright criminals.

In a recent example, the controller of the Central American subsidiary of a U.S. multinational began a series of frauds against the company. One of the schemes involved foreign currency conversion, and the controller quickly became involved with a group of locals interested in laundering large amounts of U.S. currency. Over the course of several years, the controller involved the company in more transactions with these people. All of this was a violation of the company procedures as well as of the laws of the home and host country. However, since the controller was already corrupted, the controls were useless.

When the scheme finally fell apart, the company learned of its involvement in the laundering of drug money and other illicit funds. The company immediately discontinued the practice and reported the questionable transactions to law enforcement for prosecution. The company also modified its audit tests to include a specific review of all cash transactions involving either foreign or U.S. currency for the rest of its units worldwide.

Drug traffickers and other criminals are constantly trying to recruit individuals to help them launder their ill-gotten gains. Many bribery and corruption schemes are "off the books," and they require outside investigation to identify and address. However, it is important to ensure that the organization does not overlook the various tests that can identify the evidence of money laundering that can exist "on the books." Unless the audit, security, and operations elements of the organization are actively looking for potential money laundering schemes, they will miss opportunities to put early detection controls in place.

Additional tests include peer audits, regular vacation requirements, periodic surprise audits, and regular inspections by fraud detection professionals. These cases have a cancer-like quality in that they often develop unnoticed and, if allowed to grow, spread through the local unit and subsequently throughout the entire organization.

For law enforcement and government employees, this risk is even larger because they often have even more autonomy and less oversight than corporate employees. Slush funds intended for informers and other sources can easily be subverted in these environments.

Bribery and Corruption by Your Employees

Under this scenario, an employee involves the organization in an illicit scheme. This includes schemes to bribe customs officers for lower import duties, improper gratuities to government officials, and irregular commercial payments for business relationships. Each of these acts has the potential of compromising the entire organization under the two statues mentioned earlier. In addition, they expose the organization to criminal prosecution in the country or countries involved.

In a number of countries, government officials will ask for personal payments, consulting contracts, or other improper personal benefits in return for approving contracts or ignoring currency violations. Organizations that comply with these requests place themselves squarely on the wrong side of the law, and the employees involved are at tremendous risk should the political winds shift.

Unfortunately, it happens quite often in the other direction. Salespeople, operations managers, and others initiate the improper relationship. Sometimes this is for the best of intentions, such as companies in high crime environments who get involved in paying the official police, paramilitary groups, or even criminal gangs for protection. More commonly, however, it is the dishonest individual who tries to use his organization's funds or connections to unfairly re-adjust the playing field. While some of these people act only for their personal benefit, others purport to be acting in the company's best interest. It is this group that is the most dangerous.

In this age of terrorism, everyone is familiar with the dangers of fanaticism. But remember that this can come dressed as either a corporate executive or law enforcement professional. When placed under enough stress, people will react in unexpected ways sometimes—and living or working in a foreign country creates a high level of stress.

Employees posted to such developing and changing regions as the former Soviet Union, Sub-Saharan Africa, and parts of the Pacific Rim are most likely to be exposed to the opportunity to involve the company in money laundering schemes. These areas, by virtue of their economic conditions, unstable political regimes, and cultural history, have had a greater incidence of favoritism and "gratuity"-based business relationships. In these environments, employees looking to advance their particular agenda, be it personal or professional, will often find fertile ground for these illegal acts.

Evolution of Government Attitudes

The good news is that government attitudes are changing. Many of the emerging governments are cracking down on these types of cozy relationships where friendship and position impact oversight and implementing the rule of law—if imperfectly. Regional and super-national watchdog organizations are springing up and making use of the Internet as well as traditional means to publicize countries and even specific ministries that allow or encourage corrupt behavior. These organizations publish their findings online, allowing early detection and awareness of potentially unsuitable environments. Not that organizations should stay clear of these areas entirely—but they should certainly place appropriate controls on the personnel in those identified high-risk areas.

Finally, be wary of too much success. In this highly competitive global economy, it is the rare person who stands head and shoulders above the crowd. Be especially vigilant in cases where one person has succeeded disproportionately in any organization or field. The lesson that Bernie Madoff presented most clearly to AML professionals is that anyone can launder money, and even the movement of very large sums can be hidden under the appearance of a successful business.

Official Corruption Impacts Individual Corruption

Images of corrupt public officials and others abusing the system paradoxically invite otherwise law-abiding people to consider the same mechanisms. Advertisements for "owning your own private bank," "offshore credit cards," and "tax-free income" all appeal to the greed factor.

People recognize that there are (or must be) benefits to moving wealth offshore. The images of wealth and success implied by these ads, however, are difficult to define clearly because there is no global economic structure that presents a complete picture. For example, in 1999, Merrill Lynch's *World Wealth Report* observed that one-third of the world's high-net-worth individuals kept as much as $11 trillion in offshore accounts. By 2004, Merrill Lynch has revised this figure up to $28.8 trillion, but it no longer projected how much was sheltered offshore.

As wealth has increased, the proportion held outside the holder's country has increased as well. In 2003, Boston Consulting Group's *World Wealth Report* projected that 10 to 20 percent of each region's wealth was removed from the region and kept in offshore accounts. Now, obviously, this means that money from one region is being held in another, but it implies that the appeal to keep significant portions of wealth away from government, any government, is universal.

Tax Evasion as a Gateway to Money Laundering

Tax evasion enjoys universal appeal. Few people feel that their share of the tax is fair, and many, given the opportunity, will find ways to reduce their tax obligation. Some are willing to use illegal means to reduce their tax liability—that is, tax evasion. In the early 1990s, offshore banks solicited people to make deposits and promised them access to their hidden offshore money via credit cards. Later, the U.S. Internal Revenue Service obtained the credit card records for these offshore banks and used them to prosecute various people. Despite this, it is easy to find advertisements for offshore-based credit cards today.

Tax evasion is also a relative crime in that it depends on the tax rate for the country of origin and the country of destination. If the individual is making income from legal means but lives in a country with a tax rate that is 50 percent or higher, merely moving the funds to a country with a 25 percent or lower rate can be rationalized as a prudent move, rather than tax evasion. In this way, money from other countries comes into the United States just as funds in the United States seek countries with a lower tax rate.

Although revenue collection authorities here and abroad work to mitigate these risks, the reality is that avoiding taxes by failing to record income on the tax filing form can be very hard to find. Returning to Al Capone, the lesson drawn from his case is that the tax filings must document enough income to justify the individual's lifestyle or the organization's operations. Anything above that level is often seen as "hidable" and there is little difficulty in finding programs and services that specialize in helping people and organizations hide these assets. When found, these people are often prosecuted. Thus the need to ensure that the scheme is not discovered.

Tax evasion is universally a wrongful act, but only to the individual government concerned. Involvement subjects the individual or organization to criminal and financial penalties. The societal concern is that diverting tax reduces the governmental coffers and thus reduces the amount of service that can be provided. Given the economic choices of many governments today, it is not clear that reducing income actually impacts expenditures, but that is the basis nonetheless.

Moving from Taxes to Criminal Activity

Where tax evasion is connected to money laundering is when the income is from an illicit source. It is still taxable, but it also constitutes proof of the underlying criminal act. From corruption and embezzlement to smuggling of drugs or people, few participants in illicit activities are willing to document the money from their deeds as income to various government tax authorities. So this, too, becomes a matter of relative risk perception. Given the choice to engage in illegal conduct, the decision to extend that conduct to tax evasion seems minor. The additional risk of detection from the tax reporting perspective also seems minor and thus serves as no real inhibition to the people involved.

Changing behavior is therefore tied to changing the risk perceptions, and this is a complex dynamic involving the political determinations, the regulatory remedies available, and the focus of the law enforcement entities in each country.

All "crime" is illegal. Therefore, the proceeds of crime, the compensation that participants gain from engaging in criminal acts, constitute proof of those illegal acts. Crimes including narcotics distribution, human smuggling, weapons smuggling, commercial fraud, official corruption, and many others are common. They are also profitable. When such enterprises generate

37

small levels of profit, those amounts can easily be integrated directly into the lifestyle of the individual. But when those enterprises generate larger profits, or require the payment of large sums of money from customers or to suppliers around the world, then care must be established to avoid detection.

Thus the original appeal of money laundering techniques to mobsters in the 1930s is the same for criminals of all types today. By using these techniques, they can appear to distance themselves from the underlying criminal acts, create a bar to effective prosecution, and enjoy the financial benefits of their actions. That the process is illegal can hardly be considered an impediment for criminals. And that the process has been co-opted by some terror-related groups can be seen as entirely consistent.

The Rise of Regional and Multinational AML Organizations

The member states of the Organization for Security and Cooperation in Europe (OSCE) see money laundering as a security risk and have reiterated their firm commitment to fighting the problem. In viewing money laundering as a security risk, as opposed to a financial, taxation, or regulatory problem, the OSCE correctly notes that where money laundering is successful there must be highly profitable underlying crimes. Thus, by either reducing the level of underlying crime or by reducing the profitability of those crimes, governments can impact the overall crime culture. To this end, the OSCE has intensified its efforts to combat both money laundering and terrorism financing in the past few years. Its Office of Economic and Environmental Activities (OSCE-EEA) began focusing on these criminal activities in 2001 and has been expanding these initiatives ever since.

Working with other multinational groups, including the United Nations Office on Drugs and Crime (UNODC), the World

Bank, International Monetary Fund, the International Bank for Rural Development, the European Development Bank, and other partners, OSCE-EEA has developed a variety of operations to help combat money laundering and the financing of terrorism from this security risk perspective.

OSCE urges its participating countries to achieve such objectives as the expansion of legislation, law enforcement, and regulatory structures, as well as the development of resources, both systemic and human, to identify and restrict money laundering activities. This includes the robust expansion of financial intelligence units, typically part of the law enforcement function, rather than financial regulators or tax collection authorities, which are typically administrative. This consistent approach from the security perspective drives a higher priority than simply focusing on financial implications alone.

The success of these initiatives has been seen in the rapid movement of countries, including Albania, Armenia, Azerbaijan, Belarus, Georgia, Kazakhstan, Kyrgyzstan, Montenegro, Romania, Tajikistan, Turkmenistan, and Uzbekistan, into the Financial Action Task Force (FATF) and their movement upward through the assessments as they enact more effective AML regimes.

The OSCE model seeks to promote local cooperation as a dynamic response to the entrepreneurial and rapidly evolving techniques used by money launderers.

Given the prevalence of multinational organizations, OSCE correctly recognized the potential for abuse in both the for-profit and not-for-profit sectors. Religious organizations, charitable groups, and aid organizations can all become involved in money laundering, just as legitimate business organizations can, either through the poor actions of leadership or through abuse by criminal outsiders. Keeping the focus on the relationship of the money movement to the security risk, OSCE has expanded its member focus areas to a wider range of risk channels. Merely focusing on banks and individuals left too many holes that could be successfully exploited by money launderers. From the positive direction, OSCE helped design best practice solutions for not-for-profit organizations to help them be part of the solution and reduce their risk of aiding money launderers. This combined approach, enhancing law enforcement and arming the private sector with knowledge, addresses the security risk and promotes early detection of potential money laundering activities.

The Connection between Fraud and Money Laundering

All fraud schemes involve some level of money laundering. The basis of a fraud scheme is to covertly transfer somebody else's money into an account for someone else's use. In a Ponzi scheme like Madoff's, the investors' money was laundered through the business into payments to the key people involved. While some of the best-known fraud schemes provide easy examples, the full extent to which these practices are used in fraud schemes can be seen by looking at nearly any fraud scheme and finding money laundering practices and methodologies.

Criminals used to join together into criminal organizations, or go to jail, to learn how other criminals commit crimes. The Internet has changed that. Today you can use a search engine and query "how to commit [crime of your choice]" and in less than a second have hundreds, if not thousands, of answers. Due to the way search engines work, one of the leading answers to that type of question is likely to be a blog or other posting with reader comments. So, today, if you are looking to commit a crime, the Internet not only provides you ready access to the information, but it provides an entire community of people who have added their thoughts and ideas for your consideration. So, whereas counterfeiters used to need artists to carve engraving plates to make fake money, today's counterfeiters use scanners and color printers with supplies from an ordinary office supply store. Likewise, when people needed to secretly move money out of the country, they used to use bankers, accountants, and lawyers. Today they use the Internet. While there are many legitimate home-based businesses enabled by the Internet, there are also criminal enterprises that use the same tools. Arguably, crime and vices have always been the early adopters of technology, and these tools have tremendous appeal to individuals seeking to launder money, as well as larger-scale perpetrators.

Throughout the United States, Latin America, and the Caribbean, AML regulations are more stringent than ever, with increased requirements to train their employees to detect and prevent money laundering. Despite the growing complexity of money laundering, ever larger amounts are being laundered. Why? It is easy to find regulatory requirements and financial institution training online. Publishing the rules and training guidelines gives the perpetrators access to the information and, therefore, the tools they need to counter the training. Thus, even raising the requirements and penalties on financial institutions has failed to curb the flow of illicit funds; the perpetrators are learning the materials at least as fast as the financial institution employees. There may well be a money launderer reading this book right now. In an age of ready access to information, it must be assumed that the criminals are at least as well trained as those opposing them.

While there are certainly criminal organizations, crime is essentially an entrepreneurial undertaking. People become involved because they want or need something, usually money. As criminals become increasingly technologically sophisticated, they structure their enterprises along very similar lines to legitimate companies. The appeal of working for yourself is exactly the same for an individual, no matter if the product or service provided is legal or illegal. The challenges are similar as well, with their own kind of legal considerations. That is part of the draw of laundering the proceeds of crime yourself and how otherwise honest people get attracted to tax evasion: The image of more time, more control, more money, all the same things that are pitched in advertisements for work-from-home jobs.

Money Laundering as a Do-It-Yourself Activity

It is not unusual for people to be apprehensive when beginning a new venture. With money laundering, inexperienced perpetrators will often make overly complicated systems, creating more cumbersome processes and transactions. With a real business, the systems tend to be only as complicated as management requires or at the legal and regulatory minimum. New cash-intensive accounts with overly complicated descriptions are often indicators of potential money laundering.

The keys to avoiding detection then involve looking ordinary. That is, fitting in with the existing business types—making the expected transactions rather than the unusual ones. The challenge that any money launderer faces is obscuring the movement of large amounts of money. It is for this reason that they often turn to professionals to help them move their money around safely.

The Service Providers: Bankers, Accountants, and Lawyers

As with any service business, when a need rises to the level that customers are willing to purchase, service providers will appear. The original providers were banks. As regulations reduced a bank's ability to move illicit money, consultants, accountants, and lawyers assumed those roles. In nearly every country in the world, money laundering is technically, at least, a violation. But in many jurisdictions, the level of adherence to these policies is poor. Recall the 31 countries the FATF identified as having deficiencies in compliance.

In 2001, the FATF described as a commitment to directly address the "gatekeepers": those in positions who can most directly identify and report money laundering and terrorist financing efforts. Of these, accountants are often used. In many jurisdictions, accountants provide a wide range of business services, from simple accounting through complex book management systems, bill payment processes, and even local company management services. These legitimate services can easily become money laundering if the source of the funds is not legitimate commerce but rather illicit funds. In some jurisdictions, accountants openly advertise services that appear aimed at money laundering. In these jurisdictions, the accounting firms will manage the books and records of various entities, creating invoices for back and forth between them, and initiating money movements in accordance with client instructions. These functions allow the creation of elaborate paper trails that provide the legitimizing documentation for the money launderer.

The most common of the "gatekeepers" are lawyers. Because of their role and access to the legal processes, lawyers are in a unique position to advise clients as to specific steps they can take to mitigate their exposure. As early as the 2001 FATF *Money Laundering Typologies Report,* lawyers were identified as susceptible to complex money laundering activities. Because many lawyers provide legal, business, and financial advice, and client communication is highly protected, these professionals are often used by people seeking to set up and conceal money laundering activities.

Furthermore, lawyers in their various roles are asked to attest to the authenticity of other professionals. This in itself creates a unique risk exposure. If the lawyers do not properly conduct due diligence to test for potential abuse, they may allow an innocent third party, such as a financial consultant, to engage in money laundering and thus become involved in impropriety.

Many jurisdictions have adopted AML legislation and regulations, either as recommended by the FATF or designed along similar lines. However, in many jurisdictions, the implementation of these rules leaves open the potential for abuse by professionals, including accountants in a limited way, but lawyers have more opportunities.

To address these risks, specific responsibilities have been assigned to lawyers. In Europe, lawyers are generally required to include AML aspects of transactions that could involve these activities. The obligations include client instruction, buyer due diligence testing, confirmation of beneficial ownerships, and cooperation with global authorities where relevant. These obligations apply to the movement of large sums of money into or out of the European Union, including the sale or purchase of real estate, sale or purchase of businesses or other significant assets, and the import or export of large sums through complex financial transactions.

The other attractive aspect of typical legal professionals to potential and active money launderers is the protection, or privilege, accorded to their advice. In conjunction with the above, the European Union has clarified that instructions and advice will not be covered by privilege when it is not strictly legal advice. Similarly, U.S. legal rules hold that legal privileges do not apply to illegal conduct by or with the lawyer.

A number of jurisdictions, including the United States, still do not want to dilute the privileges of legal professionals and must carefully balance the risk of lawyers getting involved in money laundering.

The U.S. Treasury Department has reiterated its desire to address money laundering and terrorist financing issues, including the involvement of nonfinancial businesses and professionals, including lawyers and accountants. However, the U.S. AML legislation takes into account legitimate U.S. attorney-client relationships as the basis of legal advice and supports the current privilege. Therefore, it is reluctant to change its current AML legislation, including professionals such as lawyers with specific requirements.

Trust and confidence are considered the keystone of the relationship between lawyers and clients. The fear is that if the lawyer is required to disclose relevant information to any third party, the relationship may be damaged.

The risk in a number of jurisdictions, including the United States, as a result, is that legal professionals could become involved in either setting up or assisting money-laundering operations.

Conclusion

Through governmental regulation, the source of the underlying funds has created a distinction between "clean" and "dirty," which, in turn, drives the creation and expansion of the money laundering services market. In a nutshell, these services are there to meet the needs of individuals who have obtained illicit income and those seeking to shelter legitimate income from taxation, creditors, former spouses, and so on. While the motives for these people may not be legitimate, as long as there is money to be made providing a service, unscrupulous individuals will provide it.

CHAPTER 3

Mechanisms for Moving Money

Money Laundering Requires Movement through the System

The definition of money laundering, and recognizing money laundering motivations, provide the basis for building an effective anti-money-laundering (AML) program within the legal framework of a country and within the organizational structure of individual companies.

As an increased understanding of the risk of AML grows, the world's largest financial institutions are seen as the highest risk for the concentration and movement of funds. Since the internal data of these institutions comprise a detailed and rich database of transactions, AML specialists see the mining of this data as a way to discover money laundering activities. From sorting through these databases of large financial institutions, it should be possible to identify the actual risk level of money laundering, that is, whether it is fraud, corruption, or even terrorism.

This is well known to the money launderers who use these very same means of modern commerce to disguise the source of their income and its origins, ownership, direction, and beneficiaries. Since they seek to end up with "clean" money and legal access to that money, they must find ways to move it through legitimate institutions, creating credible documentation, and avoiding discovery by these AML specialists.

Cash is still the preference for illicit transactions. People, aware of the illegal nature of illicit activities, are reluctant to create clear paper trails connecting them with the providers of illegal products and services. Thus these providers need to protect and move large volumes of cash into the financial sector. This initial basis is changing. As more forms of electronic commerce become accepted, the volumes of these transactions, and individual's comfort with them, are changing this reliance on cash. No matter what form the funds come in, the recipient of illicit payments needs to graft the illegal capital to a legitimate source. Every country has to varying degrees a cash-based economy that consists of both licit and illicit businesses. Where these businesses are illicit, they exist "outside" of a country's legitimate economy.

Thus the reality is that most money laundering activities look exactly like legitimate financial transactions in that they comprise the deposit of funds, the movement of those funds through the financial system, and the dispersal of those funds to a variety of entities. Since the goal is to completely hide the original source, or at least place enough intermediary steps that the original source is no longer recognizable, the most effective mechanisms involve simply moving the money from entity to entity until it is returned from a seemingly unrelated direction. For example, where a narcotics dealer owns a bar, he could deposit funds from the sale of drugs as sales from his bar and then use a payroll service to make regular direct deposit payments into his bank account. On the surface, this type of transaction would appear normal. Money launderers seek to create this appearance of normalcy in the transactions because they are seeking to end up with legitimate access to their funds.

Broken Windows Encourage Other Crimes

Money laundering has societal impacts. The Broken Window theory holds that criminals and potential criminals consider their environment when deciding to commit a crime. Where there are indicators of neglect or tolerance of crime, crimes will then be more likely to occur. Where there are indicators that minor issues are quickly corrected, major issues are less likely to succeed. Similarly, successful money laundering makes the underlying crimes more successful and thus leads to increased numbers of underlying crimes. If the funds derive from narcotics sales, human trafficking, or official corruption and can be successfully laundered, this only encourages more narcotics sales, human trafficking, or official corruption. Since these mechanisms have been adopted by terrorists, the undercover movement of money also leads to more global terrorism.

Yet despite knowing that money laundering can undermine the integrity of the entire economic system, attention and resources are often misapplied to the problem, allowing many of the money laundering processes to go undetected.

In a typical narcotics investigation, one involving more than one country, the focus will be on the development and charting of the distribution network, including both the movement of the illicit goods and the movement of the payment from those goods. Therefore, a narcotics investigation builds on the methodology of a traditional smuggling investigation, because of the asset tracking aspects. The use and tracking of the financial data is often to identify the end beneficiaries, who are sought for the narcotics violations first and any financial violations second.

Look Local, Think Global

Money movements, in more open drug conspiracy actions, are usually identified at the local level and provide the best clues. Since the objective in these cases is to identify not the local dealer, but the source and identity of the leadership, the financial transactions are used to assess the money flow direction.

For example, in the United States, one area of focus for the U.S. Drug Enforcement Administration (DEA) is the shared border with Mexico over which a large flow of illegal drugs and illicit drug payments flow. Based on years of experience in the region, the core money laundering components involved in the cross-border drug trade include bulk cash smuggling as well as using Mexican money service businesses and front-company transactions.

To address these risks of large-scale money movements, law enforcement entities typically monitor, rather than disrupt, identified money flow patterns, so they can identify the scope of the operations rather than just intercept low level individuals. This monitoring methodology provides a way to understand, target, and then finally prosecute those involved. But it requires them to allow the flow of funds to continue, sometimes for long periods of time.

While estimates of the financial scope of money laundering activities are only estimates, since the underlying activity is hidden within the myriad legitimate transactions, the consensus average is that 5 percent of the global domestic product is laundered by unscrupulous individuals through personal and businesses accounts. In essence, the constraints required by regulatory compliance push the responsibility for finding potential violators out to banking and other financial institutions. While well intentioned, this can create additional tensions because it is like asking the fox to guard the chickens. Banking is the safe, secure, and private movement of money; whereas money laundering proceeds are illegal. Banks historically have had no interest in the origins of their clients' funds and philosophically oppose being required to perform this role. As such bankers, accountants, and asset-management companies are often unaware, sometimes deliberately so, of the laundering of dirty money.

Expanding International Requirements

As it is in the United States, financial institutions around the world for the past decade have seen an expanded role in addressing money laundering and terror financing. The U.S. Patriot Act, as well as the Basel II Accord and the Wolfsburg Principles, a set of industry-based AML guidelines created by 11 of the world's leading banks, require much more enhanced AML activities, including knowing your customer and due diligence tasks.

For example, the regulatory decisions of the Financial Action Task Force (FATF), Wolfsburg Group, and Basel Committee have aimed at standardizing financial institution requirements for compliance with the relevant law enforcement duties. As these measure push forward, trying to reduce the exposure to criminal proceeds, other counter-pressures exist. Many regulations and discussions relate to the term "offshore bank." But an offshore bank is merely one that exists outside the scope and control of an individual country's regulators. While people think of Caribbean banks and those in Monaco, Lichtenstein, the Isle of Man, and like as offshore banks, in reality an offshore bank can be any bank outside of the money launderer's home country. This makes the enforcement of regulations much more challenging and has led to the Basel and Wolfsburg groups and their agreements.

The traditional offshore banking centers, however, do control disproportionately large amounts of global funds. The Cayman Islands, the most important offshore jurisdiction, is usually considered to be the fifth largest banking center in the world after London, New York, Tokyo, and Hong Kong—despite the island nation having a population of about 52,000. Significantly, the majority of the chartered financial institutions in Grand Cayman are not allowed to do business in the country; they are only chartered for international operations. In other words, aside from the limited needs of its population, the laws in Grand

Cayman were set up to encourage the creation and expatriation of funds from countries around the world.

In the past decade, many countries, especially those like Grand Cayman with limited foreign exchange and natural assets, have recognized the very significant income that they can receive from allowing international financial institutions to form.

Financial Havens Are Expanding

As the number of protective jurisdictions has expanded, countries are no longer forced to provide reduced or nonexistent tax rates to attract investors. Many of these countries, while technically complying with international standards, do not consider themselves responsible for enforcing the laws of other countries, specifically common crime and tax evasion. Thus these countries have developed a profitable business model, not unlike the money laundering process itself, wherein they provide a legal framework and low administrative costs, and the funds from around the globe pour in. One indicator of the perceived risk is that in many of these countries local residents are not allowed to do business with these entities. In many cases, the implementation of these legally structured entities provides a high level of financial security, making investigation and prosecution of investors and customers very difficult—meanwhile, the countries that host such banks, and profit from protecting foreign investors, continue to allow these self serving structures.

While it would seem that there is a strong incentive to regulate financial activity and to prevent money laundering, there can also be a distinct and significant financial incentive to use regulations that actually encourage the importation of foreign funds. The degree that a country is comfortable with this type of financial permissiveness seems to correlate with its exposure to the underlying crime. In the United States and Europe, financial regulation is substantially tighter because the crimes also tend to occur there. Whereas in the Caribbean, where the regulations are much looser, the underlying criminal acts tend to take place outside the country, resulting is no significant societal cost.

Money laundering as already discussed is well placed for the development of value-added services providers (brokers) to assist individuals or organizations and through which the money is placed. These services entities issue invoices and clear payments, creating the necessary paper trail to legitimize the funds. By expanding the number of layers through a series of such transactions, and by moving the money through entities in various countries, the original source of funds is completely concealed. Since forensic auditors would take months, if not years, to retrace every step, requiring great expense, the likelihood of discovery is perceived to be low.

To this end, AML legislation and law enforcement efforts to comply with ongoing regulatory agencies seek to identify and close loopholes that allow, enable, and encourage money laundering. This is primarily through increased oversight, stricter requirements, and legally holding financial institutions responsible for their compliance performance.

Money Laundering Is a Growth Industry

Historically, the conversion of illicit funds into legitimate proceeds has come at a cost, as the various steps in the process involve fees and associated charges. The expansion of possible venues and service providers has reduced that cost. So one purpose of these enhanced regulations is to increase the cost of conversion by reducing the profitability of criminal activity. While this has proven effective to varying degrees with many crimes, money laundering seems inversely impacted. The more regulations are tightened, the more control the government exerts over the financial sector, the more other avenues seem to appear. These regulations are in direct conflict with the individual financial motive of the money launderers. This results in more otherwise innocent people seeking money laundering services and locations, whose popularity appears to rise in direct response to enhanced government controls. This inverse relationship has been the focus of considerable analysis. Entities such as the Bank for International Settlements (BIS), Organisation for Economic Co-operation and Development (OECD), the Group of Eight, the Group of Twenty, the European Union (EU), the United Nations (UN), World Bank (WB), the International Monetary Fund International (IMF), and the Financial Stability Forum (FSF) are working to reduce money laundering. Yet as AML activities come under greater and greater scrutiny at the international level, the volume and range of options has continued to expand.

Extensive testing over the past decade has indicated that despite increased efforts at controlling the problem, the volume of money laundering may be increasing. Global economic realities are the logical reason. Criminals need useable money because almost all illegal trade is done with cash. Estimates include a variety of ideas about the cause, make-up, and motivations of the people involved in laundering. While earlier estimates had focused on criminals, later work discussed motivations related to inflation, interest rate risk, and other aspects of innovation. When illegal acts become attractive to law abiding people, the need for governmental action is high, because as the number of potential customers for the service increases, there will be a rush of innovation for professional money launderers. Entrepreneurs are everywhere. And globalization and technology have made this a universal service offering.

Law Enforcement Gets a Big Boost

In the United States, regulatory enforcement has expanded dramatically. Due specifically to the provisions in the U.S. Patriot Act, law enforcement can access data and receive cooperation that detects money laundering and leads to the seizure of illicit money inside the United States. However, this same transparency is not present in many other countries, including, for example, Mexico. Since drugs come into the United States from Mexico and most of the drug proceeds are smuggled back to Mexico, money launderers capitalize on the differences between the two counties' laws, regulations, and relative transparency.

U.S.-based authorities have a good understanding of the typical money laundering process vis-à-vis Mexico. Most funds from narcotics are smuggled across the border in bulk cash form, through individual transfers via money service businesses or even disguised in commercial transactions—that is, shipping legal goods for later sale in Mexico or in countries in Central and South America. Mexico is facing high levels of official corruption and violence from the narcotics trade, limiting the country's effectiveness in mitigating the flow of funds.

From the relevant globalization of financial rules and regulations, it is clear that through small steps, governments can dramatically impact investment attractiveness. As a result, along this scale are relative amounts of tolerance for foreign criminal activity that can encourage a least-common-denominator effect—the financial impact of these decisions impacts countries differently depending on their relationship to the underlying crimes.

Governments vary in their relative tolerance of crime—and even a small number of tolerant countries can break the chain of accountability that is essential to tracing laundered funds. Thus the strategy has to be one toward transparency, where the flow of funds can be monitored across borders with equal visibility to impede money laundering. Yet design and imposition of this kind of control is effectively quite difficult. The elements include not only the appropriate legal framework and regulatory climate, but human considerations. Economic conditions impact the size and quality of the regulatory and control workforce. Collusion, corruption, and technology all impact the effectiveness of that workforce. Failures could result in harsh economic measures that more directly impact legitimate companies and economic activity than illegitimate enterprises. As a result, there appears a significant component in the tolerance of money laundering: The larger and more developed economies have the greatest ability to act, but also generate the largest volume of laundered funds.

Financial criminals should be considered as entrepreneurs in that they share more characteristics with business methodologies than with crime theories. This is not to rationalize or accept their actions, but to provide a better framework to understand their choices. This can be argued for many types of criminal behavior, where a competent rational choice can be demonstrated, but it is especially true in financial crimes where an effective business case can be made for the behavior. Because entrepreneurial success is not predicated on the person alone, but on the underlying product need, money laundering has always existed, albeit not under that name, and will remain.

Profit Drives Criminal Activity

The profit motive engenders crime where the expected benefit from the illegal activities is greater than the perceived risk of capture and resulting punishment. By expanding the risk of discovery and/or the consequences of conviction, then the government can change the business model. This will not remove the benefit but can impact it by requiring greater profits to justify involvement.

So while governments can impact the business model, the criminals, once involved, tend to continue their commitment to money laundering, seeking out and exploiting areas wherever profitable and finding locations and institutions with weak money laundering countermeasures. The main assets of a money laundering haven are its economic services, which make for a symbiotic relationship between the world's financial centers and this type of financial criminals.

The core challenge to enforcement is how simple it is to begin a money laundering operation. It requires only the desire to do so, followed by some limited research into the destinations of choice and access to sufficient funds to make the transfer of funds worthwhile. From the most simple to the most complex scheme, the ability to create legitimate-looking entities, books, records, and the like, either locally or around the globe, can be set up quickly. Once the company is set up, deposits can be made in the company's name into a bank anywhere in the world. And depending on the jurisdiction, there may be little in the way of required financial reporting for companies that only operate internationally. There is little difficulty in setting up various business entities that give the holder anonymity, disguise the status and even nature of its management and its operating locations, and yet generates low levels of required tax.

Structuring the Scheme to Succeed

In many jurisdictions, trusts and foreign entities are unregulated, freeing them from many financial disclosure requirements. By using designated professionals or formal trustees, the actual owners of the funds can act in full control while completely concealing their identity and ownership. The use of unregulated companies also helps to hide accounts from regulatory, legal, and law enforcement agencies. Company names can be changed, or new companies created, to further dilute attention if desired. They also lead to the creation of the volumes of paperwork that mask the fictitious nature of the fund transfers. By creating false invoices, loan documents, employment contracts, and having the records and personnel to confirm these nonexistent transactions, the use of these front companies enable the money launderer to deceive the various authorities and avoid detection.

Preservation of funds is the primary objective of all money laundering activities. Were the authorities to find them, these funds would be confiscated, taxed, and otherwise lost. Thus foreign business entities and legal trusts can be set up with instructions for the movement of money to new jurisdictions if the location is discovered or identified in a legal process.

In many cases, the owners and beneficiaries of these accounts have no physical contact with the locations of these funds to ensure that there is no semblance of any connection. They can initiate a transaction via intermediaries using a simple telephone call or some other form of telecommunication so as to make any connection with their funds difficult. Should the agent be notified that official interest has arisen in the account, he can close it, transferring the funds to other entities in other jurisdictions, using as many steps as may be required to ensure safety and confidentiality once more. In some circles, these highly mobile accounts are sometimes called "walking accounts," in that they move quickly and rapidly, making legal action and seizure very difficult. Where walking accounts and the like are used, a distinct structure is followed. The first account is the main repository for deposits and many sources of funds flow through it. This account functions as an early warning tool, so that when any interest from a perceived threat is noted, the controller will have time to protect the funds in the subsidiary accounts.

Why Use a Bank, When You Can Own One?

For many years, the lure of creating or owning a private bank was compelling. By using a private bank, with its sole customer being the money launderer, any indication of official interest could lead not just to the movement of the subsidiary accounts but to the closure of the "bank" and loss of all records. The obvious connection to money laundering has greatly restricted these types of easily opened private banks, but they still exist.

In some of the more protective financial havens, only a fraction of the listed banks actually have a physical presence where an individual could open an account. The majority are operated by their owners or management companies on behalf of owners, providing the appearance of banking services.

Money launderers use professionals to legitimize their activities. They will hire accountants and management firms to keep the books and records of their entities, who file the appropriate paperwork in each jurisdiction. Money launderers hire lawyers, using the attorney–client confidentiality as well as legal advice to guide them and protect their money laundering operations and funds. There are also various bankers, brokers, and other institutions that are used to set up companies, trusts, and similar agencies, to further insulate the funds and promote confidentiality.

A regular feature of these services will be the issuance of fictitious invoices, bills of lading, end user certificates, and other types of paperwork to provide legitimacy and the appearance of real or enhanced business activities. The use of these fictitious documents to conceal drug trafficking, and other offenses, can be very successful.

Learning from the Big Fraud Schemes

Well before the mega-frauds at Enron, Tyco, WorldCom, and Adelphia made headlines, the schemes behind them were hatched during the late 1990s. It was a time of economic growth and prosperity that followed on the heels of a recession. This cycle of recession and recovery takes place again and again over the economy—in fact, it plays out in every industry, sector, country, region, and on a global scale, creating a symphony of economic activity and opportunity, for both legitimate businesses and for fraudsters.

Because money laundering, like fraud schemes, are not tied to a specific place in the economic cycle, difficult economic times can create conditions of reduced vigilance and thus increased risk of the scheme's success. Most of these schemes operate for months and even years before discovery, meaning that if you have not found existing schemes, they are likely hovering below the radar or still germinating.

The current economic climate presents a unique opportunity to study organizational attitudes toward money laundering. The economic downturn in the United States has created strong pressures within companies to reduce costs by cutting budgets and reducing employees through layoffs and other means. At the same time, the attacks of September 11, 2001, raised security awareness in general and provided a connection to both terror financing and the role that nonfinancial institutions play, knowingly or unknowingly, in perpetrating financial crimes. So which priority is winning? Are companies leaning more toward the immediate pressure to cut costs and reduce payrolls, or the enhanced regulatory and media requirements to root out money laundering?

Designing appropriate controls, implementing solutions effectively, and adapting to continuing evolving threats requires constant attention and vigilance. Too often people (and, therefore, companies) become complacent. As recent events have demonstrated, there are still considerable differences among the public, politicians, companies, and the courts as to what constitutes adequate protection from criminal activity and dishonesty.

Confronting the Inevitable

Prior research, by the Association of Certified Fraud Examiners (ACFE) and others, indicates that companies are most concerned with catastrophic events, that is, incidents that would raise public attention or affect the confidence of customers, suppliers, stockholders, and like stakeholders. Management is often comfortable pricing in the regular and "unavoidable" incidents, thus opening the door for money laundering and other fraud events to occur over time. Convincing senior managers of the viability of the threat and the reasonableness of the proposed response is especially tricky when dealing with the risks from the most sensitive of constituencies: the company's employees. This is further complicated by the clear correlation between the rank and seniority of the employee and the relative threat from money laundering. Since few executives are interested in closely examining themselves (or their peer group), they tend to concentrate on physical solutions and accounting controls that predominately affect lower-level employees. Coupled with this tendency to organizational inertia, companies have historically tended to be interested only in what they are required to do.

Since all companies are collections of people, organizational culture and motivation arise from the human needs of the founders and management. The company's culture is thus derived from a complex range of factors and may, in fact, be significantly more or less risk averse than any of the current employees. The culture includes attitudes of the founders, the organizational mission, the location of its operations, and the leading views of management, key employee personalities, and the legal, cultural, and linguistic environment. Most important, the culture of a particular company embodies the spirit of the institution. Much like the character of a man, it draws influences from the challenges and decisions faced over a lifetime, reflecting both the admirable and the undesirable. There is no single stronger force within an institution.

Balancing Security and Cost

In the 1960s, Abraham Maslow put forward his Hierarchy of Human Needs, listing *safety and security* as the second most important. This level reflects the need for stability, consistency, and dependability in the daily world. Security needs are second only to life-sustaining requirements. In the face of continuing threats to security from fraud, what is stopping companies from instituting effective defenses?

Counterbalancing the desire to achieve security is the cost of the various programs, processes, and products needed to reach that state, including the costs of replacing fired workers. Modern business practices view the cost of compliance with AML regulations as direct expenses, areas that do not contribute to the company's bottom line. Some even go so far as to resist comprehensive implementation.

Many companies have historically viewed protecting themselves from money laundering risks as a Gordian knot. They correctly recognize that they can never counter all the threats they face. Since employees are a vital component for every business, most companies establish control processes and determine reasonable compliance efforts.

Effective Fraud Prevention Strategies

Crafting an effective fraud prevention strategy involves a careful blend of science and art. Practitioners are charged with a broad range of challenges that are almost entirely measured by their degree of failure. Perhaps the most difficult of these is the pressure to deter and defend against employee fraudsters.

Thus before formulating a fraud prevention policy, it is essential to learn why employees choose to become dishonest. Crime "is just another business," a lesson that is key to reacting and responding to its methodologies. In fact, in the business of crime, commercial interests and organized crime groups can begin to look similar.

It is possible to design model security strategies and fine-tune them. However, model policies require industry-specific adjustments. To defend against employee theft, an effective anti-fraud policy must deter, detect, and ensure compliance within the bounds of the company's culture and political processes.

Thus, in an organization with no historical program in place, the properly conducted implementation of a fraud policy must begin with a risk- and security-analysis process, including delineation of the reason for change, presented in a manner that will encourage management support. For example, an increase in legal liability might be the key trigger to implementing the program. The policy objective would then be aimed at limiting the company's liability, with the secondary effect of addressing the other core issues. The implementation of Sarbanes-Oxley legislation makes this suggestion mandatory for publicly traded companies in the United States. For organizations with established programs, the same lesson holds true. When concentrating on employees, the organizations must assume that they are aware of the existing policies and procedures and intimately knowledgeable about the failings of those defenses. Approaching the situation as if the current program did not exist can identify institutional blind spots.

The Fraud Triangle

If the worlds of legal and illegal activity overlap, it would seem there is a high probability that every company employs a money launderer or a potential one. What makes these individuals, active or inactive, initiate a scheme? The trigger point can be found in the *fraud triangle*—the juxtaposition of motivation, opportunity, and justification—where an employee will act for his or her own benefit.

Why are employees dishonest? Each individual in a group of employees is likely to be no more or less dishonest than society at large. The bad news is that society at large is quite willing to be dishonest. Studies have estimated that as much as 25 percent of the population will become involved in criminal schemes if given the opportunity.

Take a motivated person, provide an opportunity, and he or she will find a justification to validate the crime. To consider how easy it is for people to make the leap, take a look at the number of cars that speed on the roads today. Each one of those drivers, consciously or unconsciously, has made the decision that his or her personal agenda is more important than the law, each knows it is wrong, and each has justified the decision, most probably giving it very little active consideration.

Having gained an understanding of the fraud triangle, the organization is prepared to craft its AML policy. But to be effective, the policy cannot be limited to what is written on paper. It must be a living thing that changes and adapts to the needs of the organization. Further, the policymakers must successfully learn from the inevitable failures of some policy feature and make the necessary adaptations.

Where to Start

Avoid the tendency to focus on those areas that are underperforming. Failing business units, missed targets, and like business problems can all be red flags for fraud, but those areas also draw more management attention and scrutiny. One of the primary rules of fraud is that when the cat is away, the mice will play. Highly successful money laundering schemes need cover and concealment to thrive. Since money laundering tends to mirror fraud schemes, look to where fraud is most likely to be successful, not just in the most obvious locations. Since economic activity increases the stress of trying to meet customer demands, market expectations, and stockholder objectives and result in pockets of insufficient management oversight, pressure is created for dishonest employees to use criminal schemes to avoid negative attention.

Depending on the organization's exposure to money laundering risks, the schemes we look for are in different stages of maturation. Employees angered over layoffs, benefit reductions, or even perceptions of management excesses have been slowly thinking of ways to outmaneuver your controls. The scary part is that they have probably found ways that will work. As the economy improves, they take advantage of staffing reductions and reduced headcount to put their schemes into action. Many fail, some are detected, others simply never find an opportunity— and others succeed. Once initiated, the statistical odds are that these schemes will continue until either you get lucky or they get sloppy. Can the odds be improved?

Detecting schemes early is the key! Keep in mind that regulators are unlikely to view any successful money laundering scheme as minor. Even those detected at low levels are correctly seen as large schemes that were caught before they grew and matured. Money laundering can be compared to icebergs. They are larger than they appear because most of the iceberg is hidden underwater. Consider the human resources challenges given the potential for corruption:

- *Fraudsters for hire.* Today's job seekers are yesterday's laid-off workers. In a competitive labor market, you may be interviewing candidates with baggage, leftover animosity from a previous job, grudges, feelings of entitlement, and so on. Most important is the possibility that potential hires carry much higher levels of financial pressure, depending on the amount of time they have been out of work or underemployed. Ensuring that new hires are vetted appropriately can help. But this means going beyond the standard background check. Too often interdepartmental rivalries between security and human resources limit the effectiveness of the screening process. Even under intense hiring pressure, take the time to conduct a proper background check, confirm past employment and education, and speak to both personal references and past supervisors to reduce the likelihood of hiring a "landmine."

- *Trust*. When it comes to positions of responsibility, take it personally. If you would not be satisfied putting your own checkbook under the company's controls, improve them. If you would not leave your possessions under the physical security standards, improve them. And most important, if you do not have faith that a specific documented policy is/ will be followed, change it. The single biggest reason that fraud schemes succeed is that employees disregarded known policies. And a culture where policies are ignored is a culture ripe for money laundering.

- *Location, location, location*. Real-estate types live by this mantra, and so should you. Where are your facilities? Consider opportunities for laundering activities based on geography, that is, employees furthest from the control centers are more likely to act independently. Now factor in unpleasant or dangerous locations. Anyplace that management does not go often or does not like to go ever, those are locations ripe for money laundering approaches.

- *Who, what, where, when, how, and why*. Knowing WHO is working for you, WHAT people have access to, WHERE money movements have the most value, WHEN the last time the protocols were reviewed or updated, HOW you would know if the organization was being used to launder money, and WHY your organization operates the way it does are all vital components to understanding the organizational strengths, and in turn knowing where the weaknesses are. Every organization is like a knight in armor, the armor protects him, but the spaces between the plates let him move. And those spaces are often overlooked vulnerabilities that can lead to disaster.

Mitigating Improper Behavior

Each company must define the limits of acceptable and improper behavior. So how do companies choose to define their position? And what effect do these policy choices have on the mitigation of fraud losses? Typically, corporate management views nonrevenue producing areas as necessary evils to be tolerated only to the extent necessary. These are the first areas where funding and headcount are reduced in an economic downturn and are often the last areas to recover after a restructuring process.

The exception to this attitude appears most commonly in mandated positions, those with specific statutory and regulatory fines attached. Flexible policies that address a wide range of potential motivators to maximize compliance rates are needed. It will be interesting to see how the expansion of International Financial Reporting Standards (IFRS) is implemented and how effective these additional regulatory requirements are in curbing money laundering activities.

Several things impede the proper defense against money launderers. First is the multidisciplinary nature of money laundering. As an abuse of trust, an act predicated on taking advantage of somebody who is unaware, identifying and preventing money laundering does not fit neatly into the standard company description of duties. There is, therefore, an opportunity for a jurisdictional dispute to arise among the accountants, lawyers, and security personnel within the organization. Not surprisingly, this type of jurisdictional wrangling does take place at many companies, with each department vying for the glory when successful and shunning the blame when not. Money launderers thrive in these environments, where more energy is expended determining who does what than in the actual doing. Organizational actions are manifestations of the personal objectives of the people who make up the company. It can, therefore, be inferred that a white collar criminal can use the company's likelihood to act, or fail to act, to further the criminal event.

Finally, there is a dire need to address the syntax with which money laundering matters are discussed. As if returning to a gentler time, people seem uncomfortable addressing money laundering as an actual crime. The need to dress up allegations of money laundering in more genteel terms further hinders an "eyes wide open" view. Selecting a context that presumes some rational explanation feeds into the all-too-common need to believe that there *is* a rational explanation. This allows the criminal or corrupt employee to "explain" his or her way out of a sticky situation.

Conclusion

Money laundering is a modern business reality. But the type, style, and success of a money laundering scheme will depend on specific elements at each organization. What works against one company will not work against another. Companies facing challenging economic times cut staff, reduce outside audits and consulting, and place increasing responsibility on decreasing numbers of employees. In doing so, these organizations inadvertently "prime the pump" for money launderers. As the cycle turns up, the same organization sees, first, an increase in work, followed by an increase in staff resources. This is analogous to a farmer sowing seeds for later crops.

For many organizations, the AML investigations follow indicators and adjust future processes based on past results rather than make adjustments in anticipation of the future needs. This means constantly chasing yesterday's schemes instead of gearing up for tomorrow's. By positioning the AML posture from reactive to anticipatory, organizations can focus resources on stopping future events, rather than constantly spending it trying to recover from successful schemes.

Finally, remember that professional money launderers, including credentialed accountants, bankers, lawyers, and other individuals who provide money laundering services, may not be operating legally in that jurisdiction, or may be willing to refuse to report certain transactions. When considering criminal service providers, it is important to allow for the possibility that they are also criminals!

CHAPTER 4

Going Global

Taking Money around the World

People move money offshore for a variety of reasons. Nearly all boil down to the need for privacy, security, and the ability to access the funds after the perpetrator flees. Given that people are trying to hide cash, a number of governments have made it their policy to help them in this process. Some of the favored locations include:

- Cayman Islands
- Bahamas
- Panama
- Netherlands Antilles
- Monaco
- Luxemburg
- Switzerland
- Isle of Mann
- Malta
- Cyprus

When selecting an offshore location, a variety of factors are considered, such as the strength of the secrecy laws and the ease of access from the perpetrator's home or comfort zone; that being those places that seem safe based on history, religion, ethnicity, or family connection. When selecting on offshore location, elements considered often include local or business languages spoken, creature comforts, political climate, livability, and, most important, the likelihood of extradition being facilitated by the local authorities.

Assuming that the perpetrator commits no crimes while within their borders, many countries will happily turn a blind eye to criminal and possibly criminal acts that have occurred elsewhere. And to encourage cash-strong persons to consider investing in their country, many governments have passed various tax laws to encourage the migration of funds. These include tax exemptions on foreign or investment income and payment of "past taxes" in return for resident alien or citizenship. It is important to note that all countries have various policies to attract foreign capital. However, some make the terms more appealing to money launderers rather than traditional businesses. Consider, for example, that until recently the country of Montenegro had a policy that provided citizenship to persons who purchased real estate valued at over EUR 500,000. Under this policy, a large number of individuals purchased "rental properties" on the Adriatic Sea, mostly from former Eastern Block countries. This real estate was available before but it took the offer of citizenship to drive the influx of foreign funds. And when the government ended the program, under strong international pressure, the influx of funds ended as well.

Moving the Money Offshore

Detecting the export of funds is difficult. It depends on the skill of the person moving the funds, the amount of funds, and the ability of investigators to track such exports. The key weaknesses are usually the points where the funds are removed from the normal process and reintroduced. So looking over the bank records for incoming and outgoing wire transfers is a good first step. Similarly, looking into the subject's foreign travel, cruising history, and hobbies can provide other areas for investigation. Few people move money to international accounts just to park it there. Drug dealers move the money to protect it and pay for drugs. Tax evaders want to limit detection and taxation. Asset hiders have similar reasons. But all still need access to their funds and want their access hidden. Therefore, the investigator must look for the means of moving the funds offshore and accessing them. Typically, once one side of the transaction is found, it provides clues to find the other side.

By parking funds in international accounts, money launderers protect them from taxation, seizure, and the courts. This frees their money to, say, invest in countries where it might be illegal (e.g., Cuba and Iran in the case of U.S. citizens), as well as pursuing more traditional investments, such as currency fluctuations and precious metals trading. Since instructions can be sent by phone, fax, mail, or computer, once the funds are safely offshore, the perpetrator never has to visit the country again to have full control of the funds.

So how does the money actually move out of the country? In a host of ways, from original to mundane, including:

- Carrying cash by hand
- Boat
- Plane
- Car
- Using the banking system:
- Wire transfers
- Business checks
- Cashier's checks
- Using professional service firms
- Gold
- Diamonds
- Jewelry

Similarly, getting the money back can use the same methodologies:

- Carry it back in
- His or hers Rolexes and like luxury goods
- Disguising its origin
- Fictitious loans
- Fictitious foreign investors
- Fictitious fees
- Using the banking system
- Cashier's checks
- Business checks
- Wire transfers

Moving money across jurisdictional lines makes tracing and, especially, recovery far more difficult for law enforcement and even more so for private efforts. Many of the financial havens are extremely reluctant to take actions against an individual on their soil as long as no local crimes have been committed. That reluctance gets stronger if the person is a citizen or even legal resident of the country. These acts, while seemingly designed to enable money laundering, are actually not that different than what every country does. Consider where the Shah of Iran and the Marcoses of the Philippines fled when their governments were overthrown.

Avoiding Detection

From the perpetrator's perspective, possession is nine-tenths of the law. And, if the money laundering scheme is ever discovered, the perpetrator can flee while retaining control over his ill-gotten gains, which are still in the safety of another governmental jurisdiction. Tracing funds through multiple international jurisdictions is possible but extremely difficult. There is no legal process for tracing funds that will not give the perpetrator ample notice and time to move the money further from the investigator's reach.

To complicate the recovery process, international financial institutions provide access to total secrecy through a variety of mechanisms, including numbered accounts, password protections, and bearer shares. Each of these, and there are others, are designed to make the investigator's job as difficult as possible while providing the money launderer time for further maneuvering. But each of the mechanisms is not cheap. Asset hiders should be prepared to pay very hefty fees for the top level of privacy and security. The silver lining for the investigator is the value of such funds. To justify this level of effort, the funds involved will be significant; thus the successful investigation will lead to the recovery that will ultimately pay for the cost of the investigation.

Currently, there are three well-known "zones" that are readily exploitable for money laundering. The following is a short consideration of each, along with a new fourth zone for consideration. Money laundering is the abuse of the existing system. If money launderers developed unique processes, they would be easy to find. Instead, they use adaptive camouflage to misuse existing mechanisms and blend in with the legitimate customers of the financial institution.

Historical Basis for Money Laundering

Banks began as individual free-standing entities. They quickly evolved cooperative mechanisms for common transactions between themselves. Along these lines, correspondent accounts were created. These accounts exist not for the benefit of a specific customer, but for that customer to use on behalf of others. Bank customers use their correspondent accounts to forward funds to other banks, exchange currencies, or convey other types of financial transactions. When properly established, the customers of foreign banks in some jurisdictions can initiate the movement of funds through correspondent accounts in U.S. banks. This allows the customer to exert control over funds in the United States despite having no listed connections to the accounts. As regulations have sought to restrict this kind of access, money launderers have made use of tiered correspondent accounts so that their transaction activities are more effectively hidden among the transactions of other correspondent accounts. This tiering of accounts is called *nesting*.

The United States is the most sought-after destination for funds, followed by London and Hong Kong. Through this mechanism, the customers of foreign banks receive cover for the movement of money into the United States. This agent bank or financial institution is known as a *gateway*. The use of these correspondent accounts for money laundering is neither new nor isolated. It is a common practice that AML regulations have long addressed. However, correspondent accounts are still very successful in money laundering schemes given the volume of legitimate transactions that flow through them, and their use continues to be prevalent.

Role of Private Banking

In recent years, the personal banking business has been a glimpse into the economy as a cause of the AML field's most sensitive areas. Private banking caters to very wealthy people with high financial net worth. They control billions of dollars, seek privacy in their activities, and resist oversight effectively. And their personal banking accounts are under relatively little control. They are a sensitive area in the field of AML investigation, especially in recent years.

Private banking is associated with potential money laundering because of the volumes of funds involved and the nature of the people involved. Private banking customers, as people with strong financial standing, are more likely to have strong political or economic integration. Sir Allen Stanford fits this description. His financial activities allow him to engage in high-profile political activities and have a very public business profile. Similarly, Bernie Madoff, as former Chairman of Nasdaq, was probably perceived and treated differently by financial and regulatory agencies than an ordinary investor.

Customers who qualify for private banking services are high-value customers to the bank. These are people who have large accounts and use many fee-based services. As with any organizations, financial institutions are reluctant to risk antagonizing their best customers. Furthermore, one of the specific services that high-net-worth individuals seek, just as ordinary depositors, is privacy. The United States, like nearly every other country in the world, has bank secrecy laws.

High-value customers such as Stanford and Madoff are more likely to receive the benefit of the doubt and thus the "subjective" aspects of AML laws may not be as tightly enforced. Since AML regulations depend on the identification of suspicious transactions, the quality of the resulting due diligence in reviewing potentially questionable transactions creates variability that can be exploited. Several commercial banks have been fined for avoiding controls on this class of customers. Riggs Bank, a long-established institution, was forced to merge with another bank when it was found to have gaps in the required controls for some high-value customers, including members of the Saudi royal family.

Enhanced Regulations

To combat money laundering, U.S. regulations call for the assessment of personal banking relationships on the basis of level of risk, by the business, location, and type of goods or services. Riggs bank was accused of ignoring these regulations in catering to its high-value customers. The foundation of any AML program is the creation of a good "personal banking relationship for the basic risk control." These assessment methods that banks use include the identity of account holders, a source of wealth, as well as "normal and expected" transaction identification. But this standard places the institution's regulatory requirements in conflict with its customer services needs. It should be noted that this standard alone helps to explain choices like those of Riggs Bank, where the bank argued that the risk from the Saudi royal family, long-term customers, was appropriately managed.

As part of the requirements, financial institutions must verify who or what each customer is, and where their funds come from. For individuals, this means establishing identity and sources of income. For organizations, it means determining the company's legal form, economic activity, and ownership structure. The range of organizational types includes governmental, not-for-profit, private company, public company, joint venture, partnership, and various other forms. Each has associated documentation, registration forms, and associated individual names.

Many more sophisticated financial institutions have adequate internal means to screen and validate potential customers. Some customers, and some financial institutions, may require the use of either specialized services or consultants to assist with particular customers. As with the Riggs Bank example, where the resulting fines totaled over $41 million and forced the bank's sale to another institution, the regulatory risk begins with the institution opening the account and continues over the life of the account. They are responsible for having adequate systems in place even for very-long-term customers.

The Black Market Peso Exchange

The U.S. Customs Service, working with various law enforcement agencies, has conducted numerous investigations into the narcotics trafficking and money laundering. One of these schemes originated in Columbia and is commonly called the Black Market Peso Exchange (BMPE). This model involves the use of money brokers to convert U.S. dollars into Columbian pesos for the intended use of drug cartels. Due to the volume of the illegal narcotics trade, this model actually influences a large percentage of money laundering transactions around the world, even though it appears to be geographically limited.

In the Black Market Peso Exchange Program, the usual approach is the transfer of high volumes of foreign currencies into local currency, in this case the Columbian peso. The currency exchange, although illegal, is done with fictitious trade documents. These will typically not mention the foreign currency parameter of the transaction. The most common Black Market Peso Exchange method is a series of structured back accounts that appear to mirror legitimate trading programs, which may, in fact, be embedded in legitimate companies and transactions, including flower importers, consumer goods companies, and so on. Payments are then made in the United States in dollars and the resulting payments are made in Columbia via peso accounts. But each transaction will come with sufficient paperwork to make it appear that it is unrelated to foreign activity at all. For example, the company in the United States might receive invoices for the provision of flowers, while the company in Columbia receives payment for the sale of horses. Each transaction appears to be independent and often involves difficult-to-track items, again such as flowers, horses, or other agricultural products. Farming leases, logging rights, and other associated sales can easily provide the necessary documentation to justify the transactions to the various government authorities.

In order to divert or diffuse attention, the use of the peso brokers is widespread so that there is no single concentration of either funds or activities. While this model appears in other places, such as Jamaica, the scale is much smaller and the illicit proceeds, when obtained in cash, are simply left as U.S. dollars. In Columbia, the volume is such that a system has evolved whereby peso brokers convert the funds into both local currency and provide legitimization at the same time.

Increasing Cooperation in Regulation

As noted previously, the Financial Action Task Force (FATF) produces an annual report on the status of AML cooperation. The belief was that only by recognizing and publicizing noncooperative countries and territories could pressure be brought to limit these activities. Over the life of the FATF, the list of countries that are either noncompliant or noncooperative has steadily shrunk. However, it should be noted that the list of countries with significant deficiencies, those deemed cooperative but with missing or poor structural components, has grown longer. There is some concern that politics has pushed some of these deficient countries onto the cooperative list before they really had the structures to be cooperative.

Authorities have asked why money laundering is tolerated in some areas and not in others. This is due to the global differentiation of money laundering; that is, certain countries feel the economic *cost* of money laundering and others experience its economic benefit. Financial disparity is why the perspective on money laundering regulations and enforcement can be very different from country to country.

Corruption and misconduct by government officials also plays a role. While sanctions may work by pressuring countries into following suit, the large volume of funds that lead to banking profits and government revenue, even bribes, provides a path for countries and organizations that profess to follow the principles, but not the essence of money laundering controls.

Thus there are clearly both legitimate and illegitimate pressures on the policies of both nations and organizations involved in implementing AML controls. To effectively reduce the possibility of a money laundering expansion then, there are a number of FATF recommendations in the middle- or high-risk categories of certain jurisdictions. Some Caribbean countries promote offshore business opportunities as a necessary component of the national economy and effective AML has limited value in attracting capital.

Since persons with sufficient money to launder are intelligent and can afford to acquire competent advice, the penalties became minor hindrances to enforcement, rather than barriers to the criminals. Well-known high-profile persons simply select clean nominees and blacklisted persons are circumvented. In the most obvious example, Osama Bin Laden is not eligible to access banking or financial products, yet no responsible authority actually believes that he has been cut off from his funds. They merely assume that he has constructed a network of front companies and nominees such that his funds can actually pass through or be held in nearly any financial institution in the world. This is the core challenge—funds do not come with names on them. Once money begins moving through the system, it is very difficult for the various institutions involved to determine criminal origin or intent. Given that this is the condition in the larger countries, imagine the effective level of control in Caribbean money laundering centers as well as other smaller nations that do not have the depth of public management capacity.

Regional Distinctions

Regional differences abound. Claims that countries, based on differing legislation and regulatory environments, are tax shelters are countered with the argument that they are merely global finance centers. Most large countries consider money laundering as an activity that takes place outside of their borders. Yet clearly such countries are the end destination for laundered money, either in their finance centers for investment or back to the launderer for personal spending. The idea that money laundering is something that occurs in small, quasi-criminal countries is nonsensical. The FATF is pushing countries to be vigilant in the movement and rotation of funds, especially as new technologies increase individual access and control of funds. Access to money held in trust, via electronic or online banking systems, and through other noncompany vehicles are greatly expanding and diversifying the risk of money laundering. (This can be seen in the Black Market Peso Exchange.)

Local innovation can have a dramatic impact on the success of money-laundering schemes. The FATF therefore has endorsed regional multilateral collaboration. Accordingly, the Caribbean Financial Action Task Force and the Asia Pacific Group on Money Laundering have been formed to address risks specific to their regions. Outside the FATF framework, the Organization of American States, Inter-American Commission on Human Rights, and the European Commission have all started programs to help facilitate the coordination of efforts and documenting the connection between the proscribed financial activity and relevant underlying crimes. On the progress front, most nations have completed the legislative aspects, so the focus is shifting to implementation. The implementation challenge is both one of ability and resources, of focus and experience. Individual countries have established financial intelligence units to develop a more effective response. Nevertheless, challenges remain. It is relatively easy to find advertisements for services in various countries that facilitate money laundering while having AML legislation prohibiting those very services.

Global Efforts

On the global level, the United Nations in 2000 held its Convention against Transnational Organized Crime in Palermo, Italy. The conference drew 123 signatory countries and established various AML provisions. This is important because it shows the depth of interest among nations—this prior to the increased focus on terror funding that would come into play following 9/11 a year later.

Various groups, accords, and treaties evince a global focus on money laundering and how it is related to other crimes. Most nations see that permissive policies and structures can incentivize criminal acts. The international community is now willing to establish standards of expectation and codes of conduct relative to financial crime enforcement. While each varies on the specific legal language, in general, these codes include guidelines on local, global, and multilateral cooperation, methods of capital flows across borders, and requirements for customer identification, record holding, and the description of suspicious transactions. As a result, there has been an increase in cross-border coordination of investigations into misconduct, corruption, organized crime, and tracking the proceeds of crime in the global economy. Individual perpetrators would appear to have fewer places to flee, and more cases initiated in the legal systems are receiving cooperation from the major offshore financial centers. But due to the variability of actual enforcement, there are still plenty of protective countries, and corruption and political influence still facilitate money laundering in certain regions. Thus, for those who want to offshore funds, there are still places to hide them.

Indeed, money laundering is actually more successful than ever before. Most required legal processes or notifications of money transfers do not move at the same speed of our globalized financial world, which enables the proceeds of crime to usually move faster. Computerized accounting systems can subdivide proceeds easily, moving funds through a variety of companies, accounts, and countries. This, combined with the incentives and tolerance that some countries have for activities and institutions that facilitate money laundering, means that money launderers can evade regulatory improvements. Small, developing, and transitional financial markets draw the attention of both legitimate and illegitimate investors.

The Law Enforcement Focus

Local and national law enforcement agencies have been restricted in their geographical scope of jurisdiction in the efforts to combat money laundering. As a result, money laundering, particularly in the online world, has bypassed the jurisdiction of many criminal authorities and has gone global. Despite the understanding of money laundering as a global risk, there is no corresponding global law enforcement agency. From the criminal prosecution perspective, there are individual money launderers, professional service providers, and global criminal enterprises. As a percentage of laundered funds, 80 percent are estimated to pass through the hands of the global criminal organizations, which can be divided into three categories:

1. Multinational criminal organizations
2. Family-headed criminal organizations
3. Terror groups

Multinational criminal organizations include the Italian mafia, the Russian *mafiya*, the Japanese *yakuza*, Chinese triads, and the Sinaloa Federation. Smaller, family-headed criminal groups are found in Columbia, Nigeria, Panama, Jamaica, the Dominican Republic, and Puerto Rico. Finally, the third group includes various terrorist organizations that fund their operations through smuggling, the sale of illicit components, human smuggling, and drug trafficking in order to achieve their political goals. While the end goals of terror financing and traditional money laundering differ, the practices and procedures are the same.

The Italian mafia is actually composed of four different individual branches operating from Italy. These components are usually grouped by family or historical association. These groups form a model for other criminal gangs in the coordination, formation of alliances, and extension to multinational organizations.

Russian *mafiya* is significantly less organized. They comprise 5,000 to 6,000 distinct groups around the globe, with varying levels of communication and cooperation. This fractured structure has also demonstrated a high level of entrepreneurial innovation. They have been associated with slavery, human smuggling, and theft of fuels, hazardous waste disposal, and telecommunications fraud. Currently, they are more engaged in online banking fraud, credit card schemes, and laundering funds for other groups.

Japan's *yakuza* have been in Japan since the early part of the seventeenth century and has, like other groups, both legitimate and illegal income sources. The *yakuza* gangs engage in smuggling drugs, gambling, and extortion, among other criminal activities, to fund their operations. Under Japanese law, identified organized crime figures cannot own any businesses, so all proceeds are thus laundered through domestic and offshore financial centers.

Triad members in China, Taiwan, Hong Kong, and Macau, as well as in Chinese communities around the world, are another example of loosely organized criminal gangs working though an agreed-upon hierarchy. Triad groups can be found in China and the United States, especially in San Francisco. They engage in drug trafficking, murder for hire, gambling, extortion, prostitution, blackmail, auto smuggling, and, of course, money laundering.

Nigerian criminal organizations have become well-known for adapting traditional fraud schemes to the cyber world. They have innovated and refined money-laundering techniques to move the proceeds of their cyber crimes from their victims to themselves.

Peru, Bolivia, and Colombia are homes to cocaine-trafficking cartels—and are where the drug originates and is manufactured. The cocaine cartels invest heavily in legitimate businesses, race horses, real estate, and traditional asset types more than many other criminal groups. Much of the money laundered by cartels runs through partially legitimate businesses and these groups have perfected the BMPE model of international money laundering.

Mexican federal officials estimate money laundering to account for 2.5 percent of Mexico's economy. This is because Mexico is the primary pathway for narcotics, including cocaine, heroin, and marijuana, which enter the United States. Since 1986, the flow of funds heading back across the Mexican border has steadily increased. Although the undeclared currency transfers are illegal, the comparative risk of returning the money south is significantly less than the risk of bringing the drugs north. As a result, smuggling and money laundering became more active. Smugglers are trying to remove funds via U.S. companies to evade oversight. By carrying check payments, rather than cash, across the border, the likelihood of discovery is very low. When the funds are deposited, along with the accompanying falsified documentation, the financial institution legitimizes the payment. While declaration of high-value financial instruments is required, subsequent compliance is rare.

Smuggling of U.S. money out of the United States is difficult, but it is not the primary focus at the border. Smuggling money is done by three different methods. Cash can be transferred back along the same path that the drugs take. Another method is to hand-carry cash through a border crossing. Finally, the money can be changed into an object, a financial instrument, a truck-load of televisions, a package of diamonds—anything that can readily be converted back into liquid funds at the destination. Border control agents are primarily focused on narcotics coming into the country. The majority of the time and attention is focused on this aspect and the attention paid to shipments out is significantly lower. In addition to the smuggling of bulk cash and the transportation of financial instruments, the third primary mechanism is the transportation of commercial goods. Since there is a limit to the number of vehicles that are searched going into and out of the United States, careful attention to the cash smuggling process and a willingness to take risk provide high odds of success.

Conclusion

The competition for funds offshore among countries that have laws that enable these activities, financial institutions that seek out these accounts, and organized criminal gangs that use the diverse flow of funds to mask their own activities are growing. With these options for moving the money across national borders, moving it directly into bank accounts and other accounts at modern financial institutions is the simplest and easiest method of money laundering. The only real risk is actually depositing the cash.

Given existing accounts and a plausible explanation, anyone patient enough can establish a valid pattern of activity that allows them to move large amounts of cash. Money launderers are adept at using simple masking mechanisms to hide illicit transactions in "normal activities." One such mechanism is the use of armored-car companies. To reduce attention from large

cash deposits, some money launderers use armored-car companies to transport the cash for them. Since this is the same mechanism used by legitimate cash-intensive businesses, they avoid
the scrutiny at "teller row," disappearing (so to speak) among
the myriad cash deliveries direct to the count room. This is the
essence of the successful money laundering scheme: find businesses that deal in comparable volumes of cash and mimic their
activities. When successfully executed, the money launderer can
defuse the suspicion generated by high-volume cash businesses.
More important, there are a range of account types to choose,
from bank, securities firms, utilities companies, and phone providers to state and federal tax authorities, casinos, and money
services business. Each provides unique aspects of the financial
transactions that can be coordinated and used to move vast sums
of cash around. And once the funds are in one of these institutions, the money launderer can move them around the world
and in and out of business, personal, and trust accounts as many
times as may be necessary to hide the origin of the funds.

CHAPTER 5

Technology and Tomorrow

The Impact of Technology

In order to launder money, perpetrators must move the money through the standard financial institution system, creating a plausible paper trail to justify its existence. Indeed, most perpetrators use simple, easily understood financial processes to move the money around (over the many exotic mechanisms that could be designed). Technology in a rapidly changing the financial landscape facilitates this movement, both in capabilities and in the control of execution, factors that matter most to money launderers.

Before examining the changes that technology brings, it is important to understand what aspects of the current banking and financial services model are important to money launderers. Traditionally, money laundering was accomplished through five primary mechanisms:

- Deposits to financial institutions, using the deposit, transfer, and movement functionality to create a paper trail.
- Wire transfers, using the instant accessibility to quickly move money around the globe.
- Front businesses, where control of the records allows the creation of any supporting details.

- Fictitious identities, "straws" (as in "strawmen"), fronts, family members, or invented souls.
- Taking it offshore (as discussed in Chapter 4).

By comingling the illicit cash deposits with a front company that uses cash directly, such as a money services business, ATM company, or liquor store, the money launderer can easily find alternative uses for the cash besides directly depositing it. Of these, the ATM business is the first example of electronic commerce entering the money laundering arena. Picture a hypothetical drug dealer who runs a rental ATM business on the side. He fills his ATM machines with the cash from the narcotics transactions. Each ATM customer then converts the illicit cash into an electronic payment directly into the drug dealer's account. Assemble a network of a few dozen ATMs in high-traffic areas and the numbers quickly allow a large amount of cash to circulate through the system, avoiding AML controls.

Many of these commercial money laundering operations are, or were, legitimate businesses. Their level of legitimacy is now diminished depending on the volume of the illicit proceeds that are funneled through them. The perpetrator simply adds additional cash onto the daily deposits, moving money into the financial accounts, while avoiding the books entirely. Under this scenario, the scheme can either be calibrated to the books on a monthly basis, or the two can never be reconciled. The only risk is that the business will be audited by the tax authorities before it is discarded. Since many money launderers change banks and front companies regularly, and the Internal Revenue Service (IRS) is three years behind in conducting audits, the real risk is minimal. Use of a cash transit company or armored-car service can help provide the appearance of normalcy, enabling the perpetrator to hide in plain sight and work with otherwise legitimate financial institutions. Since money laundering, like all fraud schemes, is designed to go undetected, the more the mechanisms looks ordinary, the lower the odds of detection.

To further lower the odds of detection, perpetrators often structure the cash by depositing large amounts only after they have been divided into smaller groups. This is easily detectable on an individual account, but much more difficult to discern when the perpetrator uses multiple banks, multiple accounts, or multiple business locations to diffuse the cash. By using a small chain of stores instead of a single location, the perpetrator can legitimately set up a group of accounts and easily move through daily amounts of cash in excess of the reporting limits. Further, by establishing accounts with multiple banks and multiple locations, larger amounts can be moved into the banking system surreptitiously. If the location is a real business, the perpetrator can pay in cash product deliveries, shifting the cash deposit responsibilities onto the delivery service and further limiting the odds of discovery.

Historically, some money launderers have used temporary bank accounts to break the chain of paper records. They open an account with certified funds, quickly move some of the funds out of the account, and then close it. Since the account is closed with a positive balance, there is no loss to the bank. And the records for this temporary account become particularly difficult to find in a subsequent investigation. This technique is still very popular with international wiring of funds and the technological advances in this method are making it more popular.

The Next Phase of Money Laundering

The move to online banking and other remote-desktop-enabling technologies makes the maneuvering and transfer of funds from account to account much more popular for money launderers. Among the over $2 trillion in wire transfers that take place every day, there is a growing percentage of user-initiated transfers, moving from bank to bank and account to account, crossing national borders and geographic regions all being driven by a single person at a keyboard from anywhere, even some remote Internet café in a third-world country.

Financial institutions are aware of the growing popularity of these tools and are migrating customers to the new technologies, and not just in the most developed economies. Some financial institutions recognize that these technologies appeal to their more questionable customers and are actively helping them understand how to use the tools to move money surreptitiously. This is a clear example of how regulators have correctly perceived the challenges in crafting an effective AML approach. The entire anti-money laundering (AML) regime is forcing financial institutions to act against their own self-interests, and, in those conditions, some organizations and many more individuals will choose to bend, if not break, the rules.

Everything Old Becomes New Again

This change in technology has also impacted the type and selection of front businesses. As commercial accounts, they can easily justify the receipt and deposit of daily cash amounts. And, since front businesses are the easiest places to layer and integrate illicit funds, using programs such as QuickBooks together with online banking allows the perpetrator to accurately and instantly control the flow of funds, rate of deposit, and trending that will be monitored by the various financial institutions.

Technology has also come to older, alternative ways of moving money around. Hawala's, based in Asia, and the Black Market Peso Exchange, based in Columbia, have migrated to instant messages, chat technology, and e-mail communications to make discovery and tracing of communications even more difficult. The absence of a traditional paper trail has always been a challenge in working with these informal money transfer businesses, but the advent of undetectable instant global communications has made them far more difficult to monitor.

Being Anybody You Want to Be

Identity theft is an emerging threat. It has all but displaced the traditional means of fake identity used in fraud cases, especially money laundering. It is simply far easier to assume the identity of a real person, complete with history, than it is to create a fictitious record that is just as convincing. Considering that the identity is not used to gain credit or exposed to loss, there is no reason for the identified person to ever learn that the accounts were opened using his or her name. The risk of discovery is low, the opportunity for misdirection is high, the odds of being ripped off by your victim are nil. Identity theft is a near-perfect solution to the enhanced due diligence requirements being exercised by financial institutions.

Less savvy perpetrators are still using straw men, both known and random, including family members, children, in-laws, and drifters to play this role. But the ease in gathering less traceable stand-ins makes identity theft the best bet for finding a name to use. When the scheme collapses, law enforcement will first be after the unknowing victim, who will plead ignorance, allowing the actual perpetrator time to fade away. Using a drifter can be equally beneficial, but a family member will quickly bring law enforcement back to you. Clearly the unknowing victim offers the best scenario for the money launderer.

With an understanding on what the perpetrators have done in the past, and the ease with which real identities are acquired, the next phase in the evolution is the leap past cash. The predominate control and limitation on money laundering is the cash to bank transaction, no matter if it is through a front company, structuring, or bribing a bank employee. But technology is leaving cash behind. eBay is the electronic flea market of today.

Instead of paying with cash, people pay electronically through PayPal, e-check, or other online forms. This means that both the seller and the buyer are removed from the cash portion of the transaction, and thus the control. If the drug dealer had a secure form of online payment for his merchandise, he could dramatically reduce the risk of prosecution, seizure, and theft.

Welcome to the Future

E-cash, in all its various forms, solves this problem. First, it provides a means for the illicit payment to be made directly to an existing account. It avoids the risk, too, of a paper trail that will lead investigators back to the source. But with the advent of smartcards (i.e., reloadable anonymous transfer devices), anyone can pass funds back and forth with no real mechanism for testing the source. These cards are already popular in Europe, Japan, and Australia, and have been on the verge of breaking out in the United States for the past several years. They require a network of "reverse" ATMs, where people feed in cash to load the cards. This resolves the money launderer's primary dilemma of how to move cash to the electronic system. It allows anyone to convert cash to a card and then use the card for transactions anywhere.

More important, while smart cards may be a risk, merging technologies is *the* risk. Japan and Australia already have embedded smart card technology into cell phones, allowing people a built-in reader and the ability to anonymously buy, confirm, and transfer funds back and forth.

So What Is the AML Response?

For the adoption of AML risk reduction and suppression, banks will require a substantial change in focus and approach. Since

1970, the U.S. Bank Secrecy Act has been the guiding voice for financial regulation, until it was updated in the 1990s. After the September 11, 2001, attacks, the U.S. Patriot Act expanded the responsibilities in regard to laundering money, specifically as it applies to terror financing. These changes in the regulations coincide with dramatic changes in technology and an explosion of electronic means of account access, financial transfer, and beneficial control.

Banks and other kinds of financial institutions need to have a Bank Secrecy Act (BSA) compliance program. These programs should establish the internal control system and specify the BSA security agents, staff training, and are specifically subject to audit. In addition, the "know your customer" principle must extend throughout the institution to confirm that the customer is not on any known fraud, terrorist, or money laundering list, such as the Foreign Assets Control Specially Designated National list.

Banking was originally focused on the care and safe transfer of funds for customers. That banks had obligations beyond their customers' needs first was implemented with the passage of the Bank Secrecy Act in 1970. Originally intended for the twenty large "financial institutions," this law was subsequently extended to all banks as well as casinos, investment firms, insurance companies, and other money services businesses. Some of the act's requirements have been extended to nonfinancial firms that accept large amounts of currency.

The single most common starting place for most money laundering schemes is to get the funds into a financial institution. As such, the primary line of defense is the point of entry because the deposit function of any financial institution is where the bulk of AML controls exist.

Since the simplest way to launder money is to deposit cash into an account, the original defense was to require reporting of very large cash deposits. Over time, the $10,000 reporting figure has not changed, but with inflation the real value of the reporting line has consistently decreased. In response, money launderers have become quite sophisticated in seeking to avoid the requirements and regulators, in turn, have consistently increased their screening tools.

Evolution of AML Controls

Early money launderers would simply deposit cash into a bank account and use checks to transfer the funds from account to account until the money is practically untraceable. This method still works, though moving consistent amounts from account to account will generate scrutiny. Using computers to distribute the funds in random, odd amounts across a variety of other accounts, however, is likely to confuse the scanning software into thinking the transactions are ordinary.

To avoid the cash focus, or create a more difficult trail for the cash, money launderers convert the cash into monetary instruments such as traveler's checks and bank checks and resell high-value items such as diamonds, gold, silver, and so forth. Once the funds are in a financial institution, they can be used to fund a lifestyle, purchase real estate, and engage in otherwise legitimate business, all as a means to "clean" the money by moving it through legitimate transactions.

Having established various businesses and bank accounts under different names, the perpetrator can negotiate apparently arm's-length deals with himself to legitimize the return of the funds. For example, international real estate flips are done by arranging to "sell" a piece of property to a business or even foreign company that is one of its controlled entities. Depending on the level of concern, these deals can be arranged through one or more controlled entities, providing an apparent history of transactions and further diffusing the trail of the original funds.

In these deals, the recorded sales price reflects not the market value but the return the money launderer desires to show.

A reasonable gain can withstand scrutiny, but too much gain will draw attention. Thus the staggered series of transactions can transfer a large sum back to the money launderer with a higher degree of safety than a single large deal.

Another variant on using property involves purchasing the property below market value and using cash to supplement the reported price. By subsequently selling the property at market value, and thus returning the funds, a legitimate capital gain is now shown where the illicit funds had been.

Still another method is making a cash deposit against the purchase of a piece of property. The deal is then cancelled and the deposit is returned via check from the real estate firm. Even if the firm charges a cancellation fee, the illicit cash has been converted into a "clean" check from the real estate company.

Adjusting to Rapidly Increasing Scale

An important feature of money laundering transactions is their scalability. With the U.S. mortgage crisis that began in 2008, large numbers of homes became available at below previous market prices. For money launderers with funds to invest, the opportunity to purchase and sell real estate—"flipping houses"—could legitimize large sums, especially across many real estate deals.

This concept of *disassociation*, meaning that the funds are held in other names, locations, or even countries, is what makes money laundering so successful even though money laundering schemes operate in one of the most heavily regulated global industries.

The same methodology used in real estate flipping can also be used to purchase consumer goods. Free-trade zones are convenient places for money launderers to use illicit funds to purchase resalable trade goods that are then sold in a destination country, creating locally bankable funds. Here, money launderers pay for the goods with money in the country where the goods are manufactured. Then the goods are shipped to a company in a free-trade zone to conceal the source of the payment. Finally, the goods are shipped to the final destination where they are sold for the local currency and a local currency account is created whereby a legitimate trade transaction has cleaned the "dirty" money.

In 2010, a toy company in Los Angeles was part of a scheme that used commercial goods to launder money. The company accepted cash payments from individuals who placed orders for toys. The toys were manufactured in China and then shipped to Columbia where they were sold to local retail stores. Since the cash payment was made in the United States, but the goods were shipped from China to Columbia, there was no record of the payment, aside from the pre-paid bill of lading. The recipient (i.e., the beneficiary of the money laundering scheme) merely had to pay the customs fees and deliver the toys to retail stores and be paid in Columbian pesos. Each piece of the transaction is clean, except for the initial cash payment, which caught the attention of the authorities.

To avoid this attention, money launderers go to great lengths to create plausible explanations for having cash, convert the cash to other forms where possible, and try to use amounts that are inconspicuous. Where they can control both sides of a transaction, this can be easy to achieve. Buying and selling items between controlled entities ensures both predictable profits and complete validation of the transaction.

The final step along this process is the use of and control over funds in offshore banks. This can involve either shell banks or accounts in real banks, either can be used effectively.

One scheme involves the use of purported gambling proceeds to mask illicit income. The perpetrator wires money from the foreign bank account to an offshore casino. The perpetrator then travels to the casino, takes the funds in chips, and spends the weekend. At the end of the weekend, the chips are con-verted to a check from the casino and deposited back into the domestic account as gambling proceeds. The advantage to this system is that the more times it is used, the easier it is to explain cash deposits as gambling income. As long as the proceeds are declared for tax purposes, the odds of detection can be minimal. The same logic is used by some organized crime groups that have purchased winning tickets at dog and horse tracks in cash and then collected the ticket to legitimize the illicit cash.

A Highly Flexible Methodology Results in Processes that Are Difficult to Stop

The simple fact is that the money-laundering methodology is extremely flexible and appeals to people with a wide range of illicit motives. Persons involved in drug trafficking, murder for hire, and terrorism rarely want to leave a financial trail. But it also appeals to people seeking to avoid taxes or hide funds from a former spouse or even a creditor. The range of people who have been convicted for money laundering includes the notorious gangster Al Capone, former Panamanian President Manuel Noriega, and former U.S. Congressman Tom Delay.

As technology changes business processes, the opportuni-ties for money laundering increase. Insurance companies, tradi-tionally thought of as safe financial firms, are actually open to exploitation. A life insurance policy, preferably one issued from a safe-haven country, can be a great vehicle for laundering illicit funds. Suppose a high-limit cash value policy is owned by an individual in the United States who is secretly the leader of an international art theft ring. As pieces are sold, his customers make payments to the insurance company where they add to the cash value of the account. The policy owner takes periodic loans against the policy value, creating fictitious invoices for services that match the amounts of the payments from the insurance company. Each party appears to be making legitimate transactions, with payments to and from an insurance company—and the underlying illicit funds, the payment for stolen art, is laundered.

While such schemes were always possible, they became practical with the advent of online account access and real-time payment verification. And such technology has greatly increased the range of schemes available to money launderers.

A good example of the use of technology is in the ability to program payment dates and amounts into online banking systems. Through these mechanisms, shell entities can readily be made to generate a wide range of activities and create the appearance of legitimate operations while actually existing only as a ledger book.

AML Is a Process, Not a Destination

For AML investigators, the technological battle is constant and never-ending. As AML agencies develop better ways of capturing the criminals, subsequent money launderers find better ways around the system. Banks are continually increasing spending to fight money laundering. Implementing new controls and processes is driving strong double-digit growth in spending on AML technologies and systems by financial institutions. Yet trafficking in narcotics, arms, and people, and funding terror, are steadily increasing, estimated at more than $1 trillion annually. Increases in money laundering and their rewards are due to technological advances and ways around the system. Using prepaid credit cards and anonymous e-mail accounts, a money launderer can exploit a mobile payment systems, creating a minimal paper trail and, if care is taken, near total anonymity. Because these advances are unregulated and function like traditional credit card services, the money launderer can readily use the proceeds.

As technology advances for criminals, so must it advance to counter them. New methods and tactics are needed to increase the success of AML prevention teams and the prosecutors seeking convictions.

Hacking into credit card databases presents incredible money laundering opportunities. Exchanging cash for useable credit card numbers can convert illicit cash into usable or saleable merchandise. And such computer crimes, perpetrated by money laundering, would entail identification theft and "collateral damage."

The age of the Internet is also the age of the online presence, in which organizations can publicize their goods, services, and activities on the Web. But do they really exist? Where prepaid cellular telephones and Web sites connect, truly virtual organizations can easily be created for minimal cost and in just a few minutes. Where office tasks and administration would require a criminal to have access to office support, technology has refined these processes so that the steps required for even a single individual to conceal or disguise the location, source, ownership, or control of any asset or entity is simply much easier.

All Countries' Regulatory Programs Are Not Equal

Technology also levels the developmental playing field to the detriment of developed countries. As discussed previously, the more developed countries bear the cost of money laundering crimes, and developing countries receive the gain from the increased economic activity that money laundering engenders. With technology, there is no need for the host country, the offshore financial center, to support the same level of infrastructure. The requirements can be automated to a greater extent, which actually decreases the risk of discovery from human error.

This is no longer an academic argument. The self-declared Principality of Sealand exists on a single World War II–era structure in the North Sea off the coast of the United Kingdom. After 30 years of existence, this unrecognized micronation leased most of its very small space to HavenCo, an Internet company that runs various gaming-related businesses. By locating to Sealand, HavenCo could secure its data from risk and judicial powers and market its collocation Internet services to persons who were equally interested in such security measures for their data. The company no longer appears to be operating, but its idea of physically locating to a micronation to protect data secrecy can hardly have gone unnoticed.

Within this context, the Financial Action Task Force (FATF) definition of shell businesses, institutions, companies, trusts, and the like, which exist only as financial accounts and registration documents, takes on an entirely new meaning when virtual businesses are considered.

For a perspective, in 2000, the FATF annual report identified 16 noncooperative countries and territories where it found conditions that support money laundering:

1. The Bahamas
2. The Cayman Islands
3. Cook Islands
4. Dominica
5. Israel
6. Lebanon
7. Liechtenstein
8. Marshall Islands
9. Nauru
10. Niue
11. Panama
12. Philippines
13. Russia

14. Saint Kitts and Nevis
15. Saint Vincent and the Grenadines
16. Sri Lanka

Of these, the Bahamas, the Cayman Islands, and Liechtenstein are the most popular foreign destinations with money launderers, and Panama, Saint Kitts and Nevis, and Saint Vincent and the Grenadines are offshore financial centers.

Technology and Offshore Havens Intersect

Since 2000, the FATF list has been repeatedly revised. The pace of legislative change, however, has fallen significantly behind the pace of technological change. E-gold Ltd., an online payment processing company, was purportedly based on the island nation of Nevis. It promoted a gold-based electronic currency that could be used to pay for goods and services. The company promoted a high level of secrecy and anonymity that immediately drew persons interested in illicit business. The company was alleged to have hosted child pornographers, narcotics dealers, tax cheats, and corrupt politicians among its clients. While the company was based in Nevis, its owners lived in the United States and were prosecuted and convicted on money laundering charges. Had they been beyond the reach of authorities, perhaps based in Nevis or some other protected place, it is likely that e-gold would still be operating. But e-gold is not alone. Numerous other technology-based enhancements that speed global access and control to offshore accounts have been created and implemented.

Despite these increases in technology, the standard of living and basis for the national economics in the countries on the 2000 FATF list have not changed. So while legislative updates may have occurred, the economic imperative for the revenue brought in from offshore financial transactions has not, calling into question the relative importance of AML measures of the various governments.

The Cost vs. the Benefit

The disconnect between economic impact and economic benefit has been raised in the AML discussions, and academics have also conducted analysis. The general consensus is that governments evaluate the cost of compliance, in both positive and negative elements, in determining how much political capital to expend on what may locally be counterproductive. Relatively small developing countries, especially island nations that have developed reputations as offshore financial centers, have significantly larger gains from facilitating money laundering than curtailing it. Estimates project that as much as 50 percent of laundered funds may move through these small countries, primarily due to the weaker political and law enforcement infrastructure. While these projections make sense, the continuing pace of technology would only seem to add to these factors.

And it should be noted that a correlation between smaller finance-focused countries does not translate into larger countries being less involved. All the funds laundered through financial centers must originate somewhere, and just as it stands to reason that smaller countries with less-developed regulatory and compliance mechanisms would allow more money laundering, it also suggests that the bulk of laundered funds comes from wealthy countries, and those where narcotics are sold versus where the narcotics originate.

Luxembourg, though itself a small country, is home to the European Court of Justice and the Secretariat of the European Parliament. So the lesson that technology offers is that anybody can launder money—the country of origin and the various relative states of development of the countries involved are not the primary factors.

Consider the Pace of Change and Progress

It was only 30 years ago that a person in the United States could walk into a U.S. bank and deposit substantial sums of cash without question. Guidelines under the BSA and later the Patriot Act have continually strengthened requirements and limited access to traditional U.S. banks. But these measures have not altered the demand. Much like Prohibition-era laws, they seek to make the sought-after product unavailable, but the laws of supply and demand are immutable—as long as there are people willing to purchase the services, there will be people willing to provide them.

So what are the opportunities in the U.S. commercial banking sector today? Banks in the United States offer a diverse range of traditional account, lending, credit card, e-commerce, and on-line banking services. From simple savings accounts to complex financial derivative products; from small town branches to virtual institutions, all run by bankers who learned their craft before the emergence of the digital world. These banks are regulated by a variety of state and federal agencies that have competing and overlapping missions to ensure the safety and security of the U.S. banking system.

Indeed, bank secrecy laws that allow regulators and law enforcement to take action regarding noncompliant banks are being avoided by going to other financial institutions, including securities brokerages, insurance companies, casinos, and smaller money services businesses. Over time, these strategies have been addressed. In 1985, casinos became subject to the obligation of bank secrecy laws, and, in 1986, the Money Laundering Control Act (MLCA) was adopted. Subsequently, broker-dealers and insurance companies came under the BSA and currency transaction reporting requirements were added and expanded. Then the Patriot Act formally required AML procedures. Banks, too, have been sanctioned for involvement, including fines, prosecutions, and even loss of banking licenses as the penalties increased.

The very nature of money laundering is elusive, making it difficult at best to track and investigate. For banks and other financial institutions, limits are set on the amount of funds that can be transacted on any given day before the amount is reported to the Office of the Comptroller of Currency. Suspicious behavior in wire transactions, deposits, or how deposits are transacted will cause alerts to be raised in modern AML systems. These alerts are researched by the Fraud Investigation Unit (FIU) and if the alert is valid and there is evidence of suspicious behavior, the activity is reported to Financial Crimes Enforcement Network (FinCEN) using a Suspicious Activity Report (SAR). Banks use these SARs as a medium to report transactions that meet particular criteria set forth in the Patriot Act and the Bank Secrecy Act. But as technology has increased the volume of SARs has increased and the opportunity for individual detailed review has declined.

Conclusion

The technology revolution has the capability to transform drug dealing, prostitution, and terror financing into cashless activities. The entire cash conversion–based AML control structure has become significantly less effective for analyzing digital activity. Add the capability for rapidly moving funds, and a drug dealer standing on the corner could make a sale, record the payment on his cell phone, and then use text messaging technology to transfer the balance from his phone to another account. When law enforcement checks the phone, they will discover nothing obviously illegal. And since nearly everyone has a cell phone, there is no probable cause to get a warrant for the account records. Assuming that hurdle is overcome, the transfer will have gone to another anonymous phone that will have transferred the funds to a card bank account, or out of the country. It is the combination of speed and anonymity that makes the emerging threat so difficult to counter. Unless the subject is being monitored in real time, actions taken a few hours to a few days later will be insufficient to trace the funds.

The existing ATM business, which requires large amounts of cash on a regular basis, is a natural place to see this kind of technological transformation in action. This expansion of the points of entry is hardly limited to emerging technologies, however. Existing technologies also provide new and enhanced points of entry. The infamous "numbered Swiss Bank Account" may be a thing of the past, but its modern incarnation is more available, accessible, and affordable than anything the Swiss bankers ever thought up.

Online casinos, PayPal, and e-money systems such as e-gold Ltd. are among the thousands of sites offering to create and host an account for you, an account that requires only a user name and password to be accessed by anyone anywhere in the world. These are the modern versions of numbered bank accounts and provide far greater functionality and protection than most people realize. Furthermore, they are often located outside of the United States. Some exist in jurisdictions where they are completely safe from governmental interference, such as Sealand, or at least claim to be. This extranationality protects both the source of the records and the individual account holders from scrutiny, while allowing them to participate in the modern banking networks.

As more people move to online banking and finance technology and become ever more comfortable moving their own money around by using a keyboard, the opportunities for individual level money laundering will dramatically increase. It is axiomatic that control structures are always behind the curve. But the pace of change is approaching Moore's Law and the pace of innovation in protection is not. As smart card technology is rolled out in the United States and other countries, reliance on cash for both legal and illegal activities will steadily diminish, requiring a dramatically different control structure to deter, detect, and prosecute money laundering cases. With technology pushing more and more "banking" operations outside of the bank walls, the opportunities for professional money launderers are expanding exponentially.

CHAPTER 6

Discovery and Prevention

Early Warning Is Essential to AML

Anti-money-laundering (AML) professionals have long known that it is not enough to respond to events. Playing fireman means that you are finding fires after the house is ablaze. Adding value requires that AML programs, like real fire-prevention programs, find ways to stop fires before they begin and take active steps to identify high-risk areas to mitigate the risks.

Fortunately, today's enhanced compliance and regulatory environment encourages this type of a proactive approach. If AML programs can seek out indications of improper activity at the smallest level possible, money launderers and terror financiers will have to find a different kind of organization to move the money through. The question is how to make that happen. Effective internal controls, a well-publicized compliance and reporting process, and a culture of honesty aid in the process. The reality, however, is that every organization has employees and customers who are dishonest.

Identifying the dishonest people, if it were possible, would be a great solution. However, until society has a means to accomplish that, AML professionals must focus on finding the areas where dishonest people set up money laundering schemes and remove those opportunities. Much like the firemen above, the goal is to not just fight the fires but to find places that are susceptible to fire and stop those fires before they start.

In keeping with evolving laws and regulations, AML efforts are moving from banking practices across the financial industry and making inroads into nonfinancial firms. AML is transitioning from a mandated cost toward a true business function, and, as that transition occurs, the skills must adapt to a changing range of expectations.

Proactive Means Active

AML professionals must move to a more proactive posture, identifying and adapting existing management strategies to get in front of potential problems, adding value through front-end efficiency, rather than being seen as either an impediment or a back-end security and compliance function. Consider that few members of management have any AML training. For most members of senior management, AML was in its infancy when they were rising through the ranks. But few company AML teams include people with any significant operational expertise. The opportunities for potential miscommunication seem obvious.

Just like fraud, money laundering prospers when its perpetrators can arbitrage the difference between what is believed and what is real. The size of the space between operational perspective and compliance reality is directly related to the organization's money laundering experiences. Simply put, money launderers succeed because they are allowed to succeed. Therefore, changing the way the organization operates can impact, but not eliminate, their behavior.

The fundamental construct in the study of fraud is the *fraud triangle*, that is, opportunity, motivation, and rationalization. Since it is not possible to know what motivates individual people or how they will rationalize their acts, the only element under the organization's direct control is the opportunity aspect. This chapter focuses on identifying the opportunities that exist in organizations every day, looking for common themes and trends that lead to the discovery and prevention of abuses.

In medieval times, castles were constructed with tight spiral staircases that were constructed to place an attacking invader at his greatest disadvantage, the direction of the spiral forcing the right-handed attacker to be constricted, while the right-handed defender had a clear view. This was the objective. Not to inhibit the use of the stairs, but to make slight changes that only hinder the evildoer. Of course, there are left-handed attackers, too; but by building programs that focus on the most likely events, castle design could incorporate other solutions for the less likely events.

By the Numbers

Frankly, when you look at the statistical evidence generated by the Association of Certified Fraud Examiners (ACFE) over the past 10 years, proactive changes is desperately needed. Despite our efforts, controls and automated travel and expense monitoring programs, over 55 percent of schemes are still discovered by accident or tip. On top of that, 80 percent of schemes run over six months and, incredibly, 40 percent run over two years before they are discovered. Since money laundering closely mirrors fraud, it is clear that the programs in use are not producing the level of effectiveness required.

Also consider the demographics on those who commit fraud. Over 40 percent of all corporate frauds are committed by a manager/executive, the type of employees that organizations need combating money laundering. The days of blaming this on clerical- or teller-level personnel are clearly gone. Other statistics point to the universality of the problem, of identified fraud perpetrators, including money launderers, 53 percent are male and

47 percent female. This means the fraud gap is smaller than the wage gap! Eighty percent are committed by people 30 to 60 years old, which is the majority of the workforce; but 50 percent are committed by people aged 36 to 50—that is the age of people often most likely to be in responsible organizational positions.

For AML professionals to produce an effective AML program, they must identify and mitigate these opportunities. So, just like the "broken windows" theory of policing, if an organization wants to reign in the big stuff, it will have to focus on the little things. Small losses, poor controls, and ineffective implementation are elements that create the atmosphere that allows money laundering to succeed.

There are a lot of lessons that the corporate world can learn from the "broken widows" model. Simply focusing on the consolidated financial statements or any high-level reports will not stop money laundering. Its processes are chameleon-like, to go by unnoticed. Knowing that, it takes a leap of faith to dive into the details because it contradicts the training and pressure to prioritize resources. The standard model dictates that organizations not expend resources until there is a known problem and creates an instant conflict when it takes resources to determine if there is a problem. Industry training has resulted in a system where pure chance is more effective at identifying money laundering than our best efforts. It is time to challenge the paradigm.

Paradigm Shift

Money laundering is based on misdirection and stagecraft. Like any world class magician's act, it depends on props and believability to keep people from focusing on the reality. Only by looking at the details themselves can organizations stop getting lost in the forest and start counting trees. By focusing on where and how money launderers get the money out of the system, we can identify the places to start focusing on that organization's own "broken windows."

Starting with the big picture, it is time to take mathematical curiosities such as Benford's Law out of the classroom and put them into everyday use. Benford's Law, named for Dr. Frank Benford, states that there is an identifiable pattern of the first digit in a random series, and that pattern is not evenly spaced. This is a tremendous tool for AML professionals because it takes something that everyone knows to be true, random distribution of numbers, and proves that they are wrong. Since everyone knows that random numbers are random, AML programs can use this simple mathematical process to determine if they are using this common, but wrong, knowledge to skew the numbers. Many otherwise sophisticated financial criminals make the mistake of milking a successful scheme to the point where it creates a measurable deviation from the norm. And then you have them.

The other tool that is greatly underappreciated is *listening*. Many courses on interviewing focus on body language and other observational elements that the interviewer uses to extract information from a subject person. This often precludes good listening skills because the interviewer is so busy observing that he or she cannot pay attention to the specific words used by the subject. The detailed focus on proactive AML policies requires the careful consideration of exactly what "is" and what "is not" done, with an eye toward understanding why. This directly correlates to the forensic reconstruction of a fraud scheme. That is, if you can understand how and why the person does something, you can predict what else they will do with increasing accuracy. And if you can predict their actions, you can anticipate what similarly situated individuals will try. Evolving effective defenses needs not be obvious, like the spiral staircases of castles—being subtle is often more efficient because it maintains the element of surprise.

As demonstrated in New York and elsewhere, you curb crime one broken window at a time. Money laundering is no different. AML techniques require less a change in skills than a change in mind-set. Fortunately, most organizations already use these kinds of detail-oriented techniques in other ways. And it is always easier to employ existing strategies in a new direction than it is to sell management on a new idea. Customer service units use mystery shoppers to ensure that the customer experience meets corporate expectations. Manufacturing units use quality-control testing labs to ensure that product specs meet promised parameters. Telephone and IT departments use hackers to test their intrusion systems to ensure that the technology, controls, and processes will protect the organization from abuse. These are all elements of the same process—identify potential weakness, provide controls and processes to defend it, and then test the controls to determine effectiveness.

Testing Your Own AML Systems

Initiating a war-gaming situation to test the actual performance of anti-fraud policies is a radical concept. Soon it will be required. The Sarbanes-Oxley Act requires not only that the internal control environment exist, but that it be assessed. The Patriot Act not only requires that the AML process exist, but that it be audited for effectiveness. The organizations that produce a real testing process will not only take control of their fraud risk, they will increase the compliance with AML dictates.

To begin, think of money laundering not as a crime but as a business opportunity. Assess it as if it were a new division of the organization that has goals, objectives, financial requirements, and resources. For the scheme to be successful, what does it need? Who is supposed to stop it? What if that person fails or is corrupted?

Assume that the scheme is in play, what kind of paper trail will it leave? How will the documents fit into the ordinary flow?

114

Every model has at least one keystone, an essential element. Identifying the keystones for both the defenses and the money launderer's attacks will reveal the potential failure points of both. After all, if the model is broken windows, then common sense suggests starting with the windows on the ground floor. Sure, a thief might get in the fiftieth floor, but a whole lot more thieves can get in on the first floor.

As part of this analysis, look at the money laundering scheme in reverse. If the scheme exists, what should we see reflected in the various financial reports? Identifying the expected impact provides guidance for the next steps in taking action.

Expanding the Business Comparison

In seeing a fraud scheme as a business, keep in mind the cost of doing business—the cost of stagecraft, the need for outside entities, and independent confirmation. While some money launderers will create elaborate staging, most will use the bare minimum necessary to succeed, such as the use of mail drops, prepaid cell phones, and answering services, to create the appearance of legitimacy. Knowing what shortcuts they are likely to take provides great insight into the techniques that will be effective in identifying and stopping them. Publication of your AML requirements or vetting procedures nullifies this advantage. There is nothing a potential money launderer likes better than to know what will be required. Be assured that they will provide exactly what the organization states it will verify.

The last major element in seeing fraud as a business is compensation. Any analysis of the scheme must include consideration of how the perpetrator is going to make money from the scheme, and what, specifically are the anticipated benefits. Materiality to a global financial institution and materiality to the money launderer are two very different figures. Different objectives require different schemes to achieve them. Bearing in mind that a great many schemes run over years not weeks, the fraudster's success depends on providing expected documentation and avoiding deep review.

By keeping "What is in it for them?" in mind, AML professionals can keep their eyes on the core objective without getting lost along the way.

This nontraditional thinking is closely related to *contrarianism*. Always doing the same thing yields the same results. As Dr. Phil often asks, "How's that working for you?" In an environment where pure chance outperforms the standard methodology, it is time to do something different. Look at it from your own eyes. Given what you know, how would you launder money through the organizations? What kinds of schemes would be successful at your organization? It does not matter if they are the current topic in AML; it matters if they are occurring in your organization today.

The Regulatory Framework

Money laundering is a global problem and dealing with it successfully requires a truly remarkable effort as the many regulations and guidelines prove. The effort of the United States is a case in point, when it began to address money laundering activities with the passage of the Bank Secrecy Act (BSA) of 1970. This established a new standard for regulators based on "suspicious" activities, rather than those that had conclusive proof. With such tools as the *currency transaction report* (CTR), *currency and monetary instrument report* (CMIR), and *foreign bank account report* (FBAR), the BSA imposed reporting requirements for ordinary banking customers. All three reports track large amounts of incoming and outgoing cash or financial instruments of $10,000 or more. The CTR documents incoming or outgoing currency, the CMIR records any coins, foreign currency, securities, or negotiable bearer bonds, as well as traveler's checks and internal bank testing for these events. The FBAR reports foreign bank processing. It should be noted that the reporting amounts have remained unchanged since 1970, when the average income was under $10,000. If these amounts were adjusted for inflation, the reporting line would be over $50,000 today.

Because money laundering is a global problem, AML efforts must be a global consideration. Any unilateral effort will only result in moving the target. The recent emphasis on money laundering that finances terrorism has exposed the connection between a wide range of crimes and the flow of funds to armed terrorist groups. The connection between illegal narcotics sales in the United States, human trafficking in Europe, and counterfeit medications in Asia is that the same mechanisms that hide the flow of profits from these illegal acts also hide the flow of funds that purchased the weapons and explosives used in New York, London, and Madrid. The pressure to identify and resolve money laundering transactions can now clearly be connected to the safety and security of people around the globe.

High-Risk Areas

The key to addressing this risk is in finding a solution to the problem of offshore banks. While all foreign banks are technically offshore, the term really refers to those banks that operate in financial haven countries. These are nations where compliance is not in their economic interest. These jurisdictions either lack or do not enforce the regulatory requirements imposed in other countries. By providing streamlined compliance programs, the customers receive legal advantages, such as:

- No mandatory reporting of suspicious transactions
- Easy creation of offshore banks, in corrupt states
- Use of U.S. dollars in offshore accounts

- Anonymous and nominee accounts allowed
- No supervision or reporting of currency movements
- Free-trade area

As an example of the competing pressures that must be addressed, the term "offshore bank" connotes specific locations depending on the person's location. While the principal offshore financial centers close to the United States are in the Cayman Islands, Panama, Bermuda, and the Bahamas, the principal offshore financial centers from the United Kingdom are in the Channel Islands. In Europe, the locations include Switzerland, Liechtenstein, and Cyprus, as well as those already named. Of these leading contenders, most are members of the British Commonwealth, such as Bermuda, the Bahamas, Grand Cayman, and the Channel Islands.

The political reality of combating money laundering is that some of the world's largest financial centers benefit from money laundering. As a result, not all countries will work to limit illicit capital, or remove illicit capital when it is identified, because doing so would harm them economically and there is no benefit. Furthermore, legal advisors, accountants, and others can safely dispense advice that facilitates money laundering without being held liable for the crimes that their services facilitate. This describes London, which serves as a hub of global finance and commerce. It is the capital of the United Kingdom and center of the Commonwealth. From this vantage, London business advisors can dispense advice on selecting the location and treatment of financial opportunities in other Commonwealth countries, such as the Channel Islands, Grand Cayman—and others that the Financial Action Task Force (FATF) lists. This complicates the analysis of size and economic conditions proposed earlier, since these "smaller countries are actually linked to much larger financial systems by being commonwealth members. It indicates that there may be a self-serving, deliberate choice to steer potentially problematic accounts to related jurisdictions. It suggests, too, that not only do smaller countries pay lip service to AML efforts, but larger and developed nations do as well.

Given that it is very easy to wire money from a bank or other financial institution, the scheduling of these wires can contribute to the layering of illegal funds that is integral to the laundering process. The wire networks combine to form a fast, efficient, and secure means of transferring funds. There are three primary networks for interbank financial transfers: CHIPs, FEDwire, and SWIFT. These networks handle approximately 70 million transfers a day, totaling $2 trillion. The wire process involves two paths, either the banks share a joint connection, then wire direct transfers the funds between the banks. If they do not, then the wire must be routed through a mutually intermediary bank to effect the transfer. The advantages to the system include its speed and accuracy. The disadvantages include the potential for rapidly moving money beyond the control of competent regulators. With little forethought, anyone can establish accounts and then quickly transfer funds through a series of accounts in financial havens, leaving a trail that can be very difficult and time consuming to reconstruct.

Money Laundering Meets Terror Financing

Criminals invent numerous ways to launder money—transferring funds through bank wires, purchase and sale of secured credit cards, jewelry, illegitimate businesses masked behind multiple legitimate companies, and the like. Al Capone was brought down not for the numerous crimes associated with alcohol, murder, and prostitution, but for tax evasion. Money laundering laws were initially developed in the 1970s to combat these crimes of tax evasion and narcotics trafficking to prevent the transfer of funds through international bank accounts. The list of those becoming part of AML efforts has expanded greatly. Not only are banks required to participate, so are casinos, securities brokerages, insurance companies, car dealers, money transfer business such as Western Union, jewelers, pawn brokers, and so on. Those involved have attempted local and regional solutions, but as long as there are jurisdictions that accept illicit funds, money laundering will succeed. Just as the French relied on the Maginot Line to defend their country at the beginning of World War II, the focus of AML controls is the initial placement into the system. Once comingled with legitimate proceeds, the opportunities for detection diminish radically. Thus the fight against money laundering is global, with countries working with the World Bank, the International Monetary Fund, and the FATF to reduce the success rate of laundering activities, support prosecution efforts, and monitor each other for compliance.

The connection between money laundering and financing terror is well documented. Terrorism has also been the impetus for expanded focus on money laundering around the world and led to more international cooperation. This can be attributed to Executive Order 13224, in which George W. Bush states "We will starve the terrorists of funding, turn them against each other, rout them out of their safe hiding places and bring them to justice." This gave the U.S. government power to impose financial sanctions on any country or nation that provides support to terrorism and to freeze the assets of nonprofit organizations, terrorist groups, entities, and corporations.

Placement, the initial phase, involves the most risk and, since the reporting level is relatively low at $10,000, money launderers have come up with creative mechanisms to avoid detection. The most frequently used mechanism is to simply structure the deposits to ensure that they do not cross the $10,000 threshold. Modern AML programs are designed to look for combinations of deposits, either the same day or in a short time frame that exceed this amount. However, the highly fractured nature of the U.S. banking market makes it easier to avoid this check. Money launderers can simply open accounts at a number of different banks and divide the cash into amounts that fall well below the reporting limits. This can work for laundering relatively small amounts of money. However, in narcotics trafficking the amounts can run to tens of thousands or hundreds of thousands a day, and structuring alone is insufficient for the volume.

Hiding in Plain Sight

The creation and management of front companies is another money laundering mechanism. Care must be given to ensure that the company transacts a high level of cash, that alternative payment types are proportional, and that the volume of deposits is reasonable for the business type and location.

To address advances in money laundering since the passage of the BSA and the subsequent laws in the 1980s, several additional laws were passed in the 1990s that addressed perceived weaknesses in AML legislation. In 1990, Congress created FinCEN, the Financial Crimes Enforcement Network, with responsibility for the investigation of financial crimes, including money laundering and other suspicious activities. FinCEN maintains the database of SAR filings and produces reports for use by regulators and law enforcement in the prosecution of money laundering, terror financing, and other financial crimes.

In 1992, with the Anti-Money Laundering Act, the suspicious activity reporting process was implemented. Here the standard came into direct conflict with the objective of the financial institutions. Suspicious activity reporting requires the reporting entity to report when an activity rises to the level of suspicion rather than proof. This is a substantial departure for the United States, which has a long legal tradition of innocent until proven guilty. The lowering of the standard puts the financial institution in the place of reporting its own customers to the legal authorities before it is even sure that anything is wrong. This conflict is still being worked out today, 18 years later. There is a wide range of reporting characteristics between financial institutions regarding the level of suspicion, what is reported, and when the reports are filed.

In 1994, the Money Laundering Suppression Act streamlined the exemption process for certain entities to avoid CTRS and established a requirement for financial institutions to implement AML exam processes. This was followed by the 1998 Money Laundering and Financial Crime Countermeasures Law that called for the implementation of AML training and the creation of High-Intensity Financial Crime Areas (HIFCA) task forces. These refinements sought to heighten the regulation and enforcement of money laundering issues involving the United States.

Criminalizing the Concealment Activities

Money launderers did not wait long to adapt to the enhanced AML regulatory environment discussed in the previous section. They found new ways to get illicit funds into financial institutions. Structuring, or smurfing, as introduced in Chapter 3, became a very popular method for moving moderate amounts of illicit cash into the banking system. For example, if a criminal needs to move only a few million dollars a year, the simplest way to launder money without detection is smurfing—the "smurfs" being people enlisted to deposit random amounts of less than $10,000 into variously named accounts at many different banks as a way to avoid the bankers being forced to report it. Another way could be by buying bank drafts from various financial institutions to circumvent thresholds for transaction reporting. Then a middleman can ship the collection of instruments for deposit elsewhere. Due diligence rarely catches this activity.

Laundering of accounts held by relatives or friends is also popular. In one case, a small-time drug trafficker had his wholesalers deposit money into his account using the ATMs. He would then withdraw the money to purchase money orders in U.S. funds, which he sent out of the country both to purchase more drugs and for safekeeping. Another case, resulting from embezzlement rather than narcotics sales, involved the purchase of real estate. The perpetrator used stolen cash to purchase money orders and cashier's checks. He then bundled the instruments and sent them to a real estate agent in Hawaii, where he closed the purchase of a piece of property using a shoe box full of money orders and cashier's checks.

Another method is shipping your money overseas. In this case, money launderers resort to shipping the money abroad in bulk cash and then arrange to get it back. Some may smuggle cash to Mexico, deposit it in a U.S. dollar account, draw out a draft, mail or carry it back into the United States, and deposit or cash it in a bank, with no requirement for the bank to report the transaction. Sometimes less bulky items are purchased domestically, such as diamonds, gold, or even precious stamps and other collectibles. There are numerous other methods, including using wire transfers, which the speed and logistical complexity make it nearly impossible to prosecute a money launderer, let alone even investigate, because of the different jurisdictions involved. Many people are beginning to launder money in non-banking-related ventures, such as buying homes and quickly selling them or doing the same with other nonfinancially related products.

The second step in the process is *layering*, which involves complex layers of financial transactions intended to mask or disguise the origin and path of the illicit proceeds. The amount of energy and expense to multiply the levels of cover and obscure the trail depend on an assessment of effective law enforcement in that jurisdiction. For example, someone trying to launder thousands of dollars is not going to purchase the same assistance as someone laundering millions. Launderers tend to move their activity to jurisdictions where there are few or weak money laundering countermeasures. One of the main resources in money laundering is the financial havens and offshore centers discussed earlier. While we generally think of the Caribbean when referring to offshore banks, there are dozens of locations around the world that are just as accommodating. The Cayman Islands, for example, one of the most important offshore jurisdictions, is generally judged to be the fifth largest financial center in the world, behind London, New York, Tokyo, and Hong Kong. These banks freely offer low or nonexistent tax rates that are attractive to investors, company owners, and ordinary citizens anxious to reduce their tax burdens.

Creating Financial Fronts

Offshore havens offer ways for non-residents to defeat the laws of other countries. In many cases, these havens enforce very strict financial secrecy, effectively shielding foreign investors from investigations and prosecutions from their home countries. Any reasonably intelligent money launderer wanting to stay out of prison will establish a bank account in at least one financial haven. Often these accounts will be created in the name of a corporation rather than as an individual. Sometimes it will just be a numbered account. In order to increase the appearance of legitimacy, it is preferable that such a company already have a history of actual activity. This is where legal advice can readily pay off. Some of these attorneys and business advisors have a literal shelf of companies already in existence and, instead of being created or purchased, are merely rented for a specific time period or transaction. Then the company is allowed to go back to a regular level of activity, minimizing detection, as all records indicate it to be a long-standing entity with historical records.

Once the corporation is set up or acquired, a bank deposit is then made in the haven country in the name of that offshore company. By doing this, it makes it appear that high-profit transactions are legitimate enough to avoid the attention of the regulators in either country. The incentive for businesses to be registered in offshore havens is to escape the severe tax and registration regulations on domestic companies. They can funnel large amounts of capital to and from offshore countries without the need to declare the transactions to domestic fiscal authorities. On the condition that it do no business where it is established, an international business or offshore corporation enables its owners to act with complete anonymity and not pay taxes. In many jurisdictions, it is not even required to keep corporate books or records and thus is perfect for concealing the origin and destination of goods in international commerce. Companies can even be capitalized with bearer shares, so, while there is no owner on record anywhere, the person who physically possesses the share certificates owns the company.

Keeping the Money Moving

Regulators have long been suspicious of what they call *walking accounts*, accounts that are set up to avoid compliance with legal requirements. For instance, criminals will open an account in one jurisdiction but with instructions for any incoming funds to be transferred immediately to another location. Additionally, the bank will be instructed, in the event of inquiries, that bank officials in the second location be informed. Once they are informed, they in turn have instructions to transfer the money elsewhere. These schemes pose serious problems for tracking and seizing dirty money. The first account is simply the initial depository, and money moves in and then immediately moves out. The function of the account is, essentially, to act as an early-warning mechanism to identify any inquiries by law enforcement and to set off further countermeasures to protect the money.

An experienced money launderer will use intermediaries such as lawyers along the money laundering route so that they have the protection of the lawyer–client relationship. There is also an increasing reliance in offshore centers on brokers and agents to generate customers to act as intermediaries in establishing accounts, trusts, and the like, and to act as an additional layer of insulation and confidentiality. These professional launderers include accountants, lawyers, and private bankers who, while offering money laundering services to a wide range of criminals, are adept at not asking questions that would require them to refuse business or even to report their clients or potential clients to the authorities. The risk for these professional money launderers in providing these services is that failing to comply with professional best standards might create liability for their clients' illicit acts. Some offshore financial institutions will generate false invoices, bills of lading, end-user certificates, and other forms of documentation to give the appearance of legitimacy to a variety of illicit transactions. Over-invoicing using false documents can be an excellent cover for moving the proceeds of drug trafficking and other crimes, while false invoices, bills, and receipts can be used for a variety of tax frauds.

As AML provisions increased, pressure to be more cautious with U.S. records resulted in locally based service providers emerging. Under current regulations, U.S. financial institutions now maintain copies of the account information with any bank notes. And the obligation to keep these records, which exist for all customers, is strengthened for accounts owned or controlled by foreign persons or entities. The records must include the title and foreign organization's name and contact details, as well as the same information for the owner or U.S. resident.

Keeping the Tax Man Happy

Bear in mind that money laundering is done so that a criminal or criminal organization can receive the illicit income while avoiding the collateral problems of taxable income, especially those that lead to charges of tax evasion and arrest. The goal then is to repatriate reportable income, funds from sources that will both withstand scrutiny and avoid suspicion. U.S. organized crime groups have learned this lesson. Money laundering is used because a criminal has to show a source of income to account for any disparities between income and lifestyle. If the reported income is $10,000, but the person lives in a $1 million home, it will encourage suspicion. But if that same person shows $500,000 income, the possibility of hidden income is diminished, at least in the eyes of the authorities.

Criminals considering money laundering typically have considerable income to shelter—funds generated from various criminal activities such as drug trafficking, prostitution, extortion, fencing stolen goods, and the like, even no-show jobs. Historically, individuals simply comingled the illicit funds with legitimate income, but today forensic accountants are adept at reconstructing books and records. This will still work if the amount in question is minor. Then there is virtually no way of tracking it. If you have a larger income, you would have to create a business that would disguise the difference between real and fake income.

For example, a bar or restaurant would be a good choice to launder money because the cash sales can readily be adjusted. However, the limitation is that total sales must relate to inventory purchased; if an audit determined that the sales receipts did not balance to the liquor and food purchases, that will generate suspicion and focus unwanted official attention. Better choices involve businesses that are service-oriented or have inventories that are difficult to trace. Car washes, parking lots, religious establishments, these are very difficult to test for sales accuracy. Again the purpose here is to show sufficient income to appease the tax authorities and blend into normal life. Only in television and the movies do the fictional money launderers enjoy a high profile. In the real world, they seek to be invisible because any attention can bring unwanted attention.

Most modern-day money laundering begins with the efforts to hide illicit funds from view. This may be because of official corruption or illegal narcotics; it may be the resultant embezzlement of a pending divorce. Begin with the assumption that the person has taken the easiest course of action. Most people will keep initial proceeds close to them, so consider the possibility of cash hidden in the home, or the use of a safe deposit box at a bank or vault company. From there, consider the possibility and offshore locations and the means to move the money there.

Successfully laundering the money is always a two-part process, with the first part removing the illicit funds and the second part returning the legitimized funds. Investigating money laundering can begin at either end. In fact, it is arguably easier to prove money laundering upon the return, as that clarifies the location question. Knowing where the funds returned from provides a locus for investigation to determine how the funds got there in the first place.

Another form of money laundering involved overbilling through an import/export business. By acting as both buyer and seller, the perpetrator can control the direction and flow of funds and be assured that all of the resulting paperwork will balance. Further, while involving innocent third parties can provide a greater appearance of legitimacy, it also exposes the scheme to discovery.

Conclusion

The principal challenge to preventing, detecting, and investigating money laundering is that the various activities, if conducted with some forethought are easy to accomplish. Recall that money laundering, at its simplest, is the act of making money that comes from Source "A" look like it comes from Source "B." In practice, criminals are trying to disguise the origins of money obtained through illegal activities, so it looks like it was obtained from legal sources. As simple as that sounds, finding the individual laundering transactions in the volume of legitimate transactions can be extremely difficult.

Money laundering is a business. It operates by the same rules and motivations as all other businesses. By considering fraudsters from an entrepreneurial perspective, AML professionals are better able to see where they are going. This is one of those instances where knowledge is truly power. Since the perpetrator is constantly educated by the media, other fraudsters, and even government organizations, AML professionals must move beyond a response-based model, taking the leap to operational involvement to make AML programs successful. Like every other mimic, the fraudster depends on only having to survive a cursory review. He is unable to sustain serious scrutiny. So discovery and prevention must be based on serious scrutiny of all minor violations, to create a climate where major violations leap off the page and are not obscured by the myriad of minor issues. As demonstrated in the broken windows theory of policing, there are no victimless crimes. There are only those that lead to conditions where major crime is more likely to occur.

CHAPTER 7

Terror Financing

Terrorists Use Money Laundering Techniques

The September 11 terror attacks on the World Trade Center and Pentagon forced a major change in anti-money laundering (AML) enforcement. The first was legislative, in the creation of the Patriot Act; the second was perspective, in the change in direction with the resolution of financial crimes being addressed from a combined and international perspective. While the regulations to this point addressed crime, criminal proceeds, and U.S.-registered financial institutions, that changed with the Patriot Act and it took a new direction. The Act required the creation, and independent auditing, of a specific AML function. The Act further restricted U.S. financial institutions from conducting business with foreign shell banks, known terrorists, and required knowing-your-customer provisions and authorized extensive information sharing with law enforcement.

The ability to launder money has allowed terrorist groups spanning the globe the ability to fund their operations with clean money and not be detected by authorities. Concealing the identity, source, or destination of illegally gained money is important to terrorists, not only for money-laundered funding of standard operations. It also prevents authorities from learning about car bombs, attacks on civilians, airplane hijacking, and the like.

As money laundering at the global level became the focus, international associations have been formed to promote the settlement of this issue. Many countries are very open in concept, and the implementation issues have already been discussed. A register by individual governments cannot help to prevent the money laundering schemes around the world. Instead, the co-ordination of the Financial Action Task Force has resulted in a surge of standardization of policies and legal framework to combat money laundering and terrorist financing. Money laundering and terrorist financing are the two financial vices that perpetually threaten the global financial markets. To analyze the risks of these two related issues, they should be separated for greater clarity.

Similarities and Distinctions

While money laundering has been defined previously and discussed in depth, all prior discussions have revolved around the conversion of the proceeds from crime through the financial markets to emerge in a more legitimate form. However, terror financing is simply the funding mechanism for acts of terror by people who share the same political aspirations and ideologies. Terrorists form part of an underground network with a common goal to cause shock, trauma, political communication, financial disruption, and destabilization of the system.

So how is it that two totally different kinds of issues are so closely related in terms of activities? It is worth bringing out the difference between money laundering and terror financing. The differences are merely those of the intent of the end user; the practices are the same. The obscuring of the true flow of funds is the same. While the source for terror financing is not always an underlying criminal act, it usually is. The only distinct difference is the size of the transactions. Terror financing requires substantially smaller amounts of money than narcotics trafficking or other common predicate crimes for money launder-ing. This was the huge change in direction after September 11, 2001, the shift to tools that can find patterns at much smaller lev-els and in much smaller increments. Whereas traditional money launderers might be looking to move million or tens of millions of dollars, terror financing might be trying to move tens of thou-sands or even hundreds of thousands.

The very first is the "placement" stage, where the proceeds of the crime, usually cash, are placed into the financial system. Ter-ror financing faces the same challenge, perhaps even more so. Terrorists are much more likely to be on banned lists than other kinds of criminals. Successfully creating an entity and getting an account opened with a financial institution is much more difficult for these groups. The result is that they will use *nominees*. While financial institutions are alert for potential nominee accounts of other financial misdeed, very few are focused on these kinds of accounts that contain such relatively small amounts of money.

This is the actual act of moving ill-gotten wealth into the financial system. To the criminals, it is the riskiest and most time-consuming stage, as it involves the breaking down of the quantity of cash into smaller amounts in order to get it deposited in banks without raising any suspicions. Again, this step involves less money in terror financing cases, so the challenges are corre-spondingly lower.

Application of the Methodology to Terror Financing

Traditionally, placement is always referred to in terms of cash, but this is not the case. Proceeds derived from high-value frauds and extortion may arrive in more complex methods of transfers rather than cash. These sorts of transactions are also another form of placement. One of the techniques is for the criminal to employ many people to pay unsuspicious petty amounts of money into numerous bank accounts. The people employed by the criminal are called "smurfs," discussed in Chapter 6. The same process of placement could be carried out in casinos, or by purchase of winning lottery tickets and other assets.

For terror financing, it can be as easy as paying groups of people who collectively wire funds to a single account. It is not unusual for this consolidation account to bear the name of a charitable or aid organization. That way if anyone reviews the activity, they will see lots of different named accounts making relatively small "donations." This kind of expected behavior reduces suspicion. Terror financing groups will also go to some effort to build a connection between the origination of the funds and the destination. For example, Saudi Arabia is well known for funding schools and community centers. Were an account to be opened in the name of a new religious school and receive donations in the name of various schools and people in Saudi Arabia, the foreign inflow of deposits would raise attention. If each deposit was small enough and the aggregate remained relatively low, it is unlikely to generate special attention. This is the intention of the terror funding groups; by mimicking legitimate actions terrorist can hide the flow of funds to their illicit activities.

Next is the layering stage, where proceeds are moved through a series of complex transactions involving movement from different assets and jurisdiction in a bid to erase all traces of their origins. This is a complex financial transaction that requires expertise. As a matter of fact, hardcore criminals have less time and experience required for such expertise involved in the layering process. These criminals generally employ highly skilled professionals in the legal and financial industries. These professionals use their knowledge to evade the law and identify jurisdictions with weak controls and strict secrecy laws. As mentioned in previous chapters, professionals such as lawyers, accountants, and bankers are involved in these shady dealings, as the rewards are huge and tempting. They are professionals inside the financial and legal system; as such, they have a high-level mastery over the loopholes legislators leave in AML regulations.

Osama Bin Laden is wealthy. What his financial status is today is unknown, but it can be assumed that he does not have funds in a bank under his name. He is going to go to great lengths to ensure that his hidden accounts cannot be traced back to him from any specific terror event. So to that end, it is reasonable to hypothesize that Osama Bin Laden would use a complicated series of transactions to move money from whatever accounts he has control over to the various terror operations. His methods are precisely like those of the narcotics smuggler, obscuring the beginning and the end of each transaction from each other.

The third and final stage is the integration stage, where the money returns, legitimized, to commerce. The money at this stage now enters the financial system as legitimate earnings of an individual or company. Although it is difficult to identify laundered money at this stage, suspicions may be raised through concentration of wire transfers across boundaries. Furthermore, if law enforcement gets wind of a bank's possible involvement in money laundering, the authorities may start to scrutinize the bank's activities and uncover large operations in that way. While suspicions about the origins may be more apparent with terror financing, this stage is very similar. The end result is that the funds will be transferred into the account of the weapons dealer, bomb supplier, or terror team in ways and amounts that make detection unlikely. It is always possible that a practice, policy, or procedure will generate some reasonable suspicion that can be acted on, but given the amounts involved in terror financing, it is far less likely.

Global Impact of Financial Crimes

Money laundering is seen as creating dangers beyond the individual countries. Compromising with money launderers will mean encouraging their criminal activities, which aggregate these huge sums of money from small, individual transactions. Money laundering is the first serious crime that can be directly related to global economic matters. More than any other reason, this explains why its emergence has coincided with the advent of globalization. The risk of money laundering on the global financial system parallels the risks of terror financing.

Of the four leading prevention strategies, each applies to terror financing:

- The efforts of individual countries to limit money laundering, if implemented properly should be effective at the discovery, identification, and resolution of money laundering. Similarly, the fair implementation of these controls and procedures should limit terror groups' abilities to both raise and distribute funds.

- Legislation must be enacted to prevent money laundering through national financial systems. Where this legislation is enacted and implemented, terror groups will be similarly impacted. While traditional money launderers are only motivated by profit or greed, terror financing has a political agenda. So the potential for individual corruption changes. AML systems look for the impact of bribery or corruption of financial institution personnel. With terror financing, the risk expands to include collusion not through corruption, but through political sympathies. Seeking those connections is much more difficult than risks of simple corruption.

- Combating the global illegal narcotics trade will have a resulting impact on money laundering, as this is the principal driver of the activity. The consensus for a global response to terrorism is less clear. While illegal narcotics involve crimes in all countries, the penalties vary from lax to severe. With terrorism, the responses range from active support to active combat. Unless there is a truly global response to acts of terror, it can be readily anticipated that the money funding terror will find a home.

- The laws, regulations, and guidelines for international assistance should be integrated into national criminal procedures. Herein a nation's law enforcement entities are limited in both the assistance they can provide and accept regarding potential acts of terror. There seems to be a division between these two aspects. Most countries will quite readily accept information about acts that are to occur in them, but are much less vigilant if it looks like attacks are aimed elsewhere, even if they are involved in the flow of funds, arms, or support for that attack. The range of political support for terror acts is directly tied to the political position of the targets of terror. For example, the regional issues resulting from terror tactics in the Middle East are well known, yet the support, both overt and financial, for terror groups that target Israel is quite high. These groups fit within the regional political views of the day. The fact that they serve to destabilize the neighboring countries as well appears to hold less importance than who their primary target is.

Alternative Laundering Mechanisms

When terror groups fear attention from traditional banking systems, they use alternative models of money laundering. The most common alternative remittance system is *hawala*, a form of traditional money movement from Southeast Asia. Under this system, funds are moved through networks of trusted associates, often family members. It can be described as banking without records. Participants use trust and code words to authorize each other to release funds, without having corresponding fund transfers between themselves. So, in this regard, it is like a bank debiting a customer account without sending a complimentary wire to the branch that issued the cash. The attraction of a system of global banking that operates without records should be obvious.

Hawalas transact billions of dollars without records. While these originated as banking substitutes in regions without banking structures, their use today demonstrates the value of secrecy. Every country has a bank secrecy law or equivalent legislation. The extent and penalties of the secrecy provided may vary, but the underlying commitment to customer secrecy has been universal until the advent of AML laws. Persons in possession of illicit funds may fear that disclosure will eventually lead to prosecution and imprisonment. Thus the launderer is prepared to pay a high price for secrecy. If secrecy is removed, then the money launderer, due to risk of disclosure, will seek alternative means. If the money launderer is concerned about disclosure and legal consequences, the terror financer is concerned about the mission being disrupted. So, while use of alternative systems may involve costs and risk of theft, criminals have ways of ensuring that their funds are handled properly. Stealing from either narcotics traffickers or terror groups would have strong negative consequences.

The Chechen conflict illustrates the challenges of terror financing. Despite being named a terror group by the European Union, the various groups in Chechnya combined to obtain $800 million a year in overseas "donations," exacerbating, if not outright funding, the conflict with Russia. The flow of funds from supportive entities and organizations around the world were funneled through various banks and financial institutions. While none of the accounts stated outright that the funds were intended for terrorism, that volume of funds flowing into a war zone should have indicated some concern.

While Russia was complaining of external funding, there was also internal funding. Some individuals in Moscow began selling counterfeit products. The proceeds of this crime were directed among three subsidiary businesses, each using a Moscow commercial bank account. From there, the funds were relieved either by transfer to a second account or by direct withdrawal. In both cases, the funds were ultimately delivered to groups in opposition to the Russian Federation. Where the funds were withdrawn directly, they were couriered to Chechnya, where they were transferred to additional bank accounts in the United States and Poland. The transfers went from Russia to the United States and then on to Poland, where they were ultimately extracted and delivered to the groups in Chechnya.

While demonstrating the connection between underlying crime, money laundering, and terror financing, there are two important aspects of this case for further consideration. First, there is a ready market for the cash-carrying "business." The transport of bulk cash is a highly active role, involving mostly major currencies that are common to terror financing. Second, subsequent investigation determined that the underlying Moscow bank accounts were opened on the basis of forged documents. This case illustrates the extent of the global cross-connection between crime and terror financing—and the fund-raising that facilitates the latter.

Regulatory Responses

An effective AML posture is vital. Membership in the Financial Action Task Force (FATF) and successful implementation of its programs become important pieces in the resolution of terrorist financing vis-à-vis money laundering. To become part of the FATF, minimum standards have to be met:

- Commitment to prevent money laundering in the political year.
- Adoption of proposals within three years.
- Annual self-assessment activities.
- Must be diligent in participation and effort.
- Must be a strategic effort.
- Money laundering and drug trafficking should be unlawful.

- Financial institutions form the front line of defense and must have policies and practices that discern between legitimate transactions and report suspicious transactions.

FATF, in turn, can provide assistance, guidelines, investigative training, and support to encourage the robust development of global AML measures. Since the FATF has successfully recruited nearly every country in the world into its membership, active money laundering and terror financing efforts should be diminishing. But the FATF publications suggest that too many countries signed on to the principles but lag in policy implementation. Naming, listing, and publishing information about the lack of cooperation or commitment on the part of these nations provides a mechanism for shaming them into compliance. However, it also provides a road map for persons seeking safe jurisdictions.

Thus, mere membership and even legal structures are insufficient. A look back over the continuing legislation indicates that effectively combating money laundering and terror financing will require successively diminishing financial privacy to ensure compliance. Whether this is politically palatable has yet to be seen.

The connection between policy and implementation was directly addressed in 1999 at the Financial Stability Forum. By that time, many of the older offshore financial centers had joined FATF. Yet the results were less than anticipated. In 2002, the International Monetary Fund (IMF) and World Bank began to study the coordination of the challenges of global money laundering measures. This resulted in over 100 countries responding to the call to share information to help build programs that effectively combat money laundering and terrorist financing. Under the IMF and World Bank, this program seeks to coordinate information by enabling countries to register their guidelines and the promotion of global coordination between government departments.

Conclusion

In the time frame that multinational organizations worked to re-solve this disconnect between agreements and action, another approach was also undertaken. While global organizations were concerned about national participation, the banking regulators were concerned about individual financial institution participation. The Wolfsburg Group created a set of bank-based guidelines as the basis for an effective AML program. The principles are voluntary and more like banking best practices than regulatory demands—that is, the approach is from the banking perspective. Subsequently, in 2002, the Wolfsburg Group issued guidelines to address terror financing. Then, in 2003, it expanded the guidelines to cover due diligence, including the supervision, inspection, and background research of customers who could be involved in either money laundering or terror financing.

Building on these efforts, the Basel Capital Accords promoted guidelines for a wide range of banking activities. These approached the money laundering and terror financing issue from a risk-based perspective. These accords provide guidance to reduce policy failure because of inadequate or failed internal methods, producers, and programs and from external events. In regard to money laundering, the program risk is most important. If the "know your customer" approach and compliance obligations are not given sufficient value and commitment, then the likelihood of money laundering and terror financing increase.

CHAPTER 8

Identifying Risk Exposures

AML Exposures: Assessing Financial Institution Risk

In today's multinational business climate, exposures to money laundering fraud exist despite the best anti-money-laundering (AML) measures. What do you need to do to ensure that you and your team are prepared to identify and resolve AML risks in the information age? Are you prepared to tackle global issues such as privacy, cultural idiosyncrasies, and changing legal standards that can make a clear determination of what is a legal transaction and money laundering—which depends on the countries involved?

Resolving allegations and potential AML issues in today's business climate means AML professionals face an ever-broadening range of investigative realities. Customers, employees, and business partners are more often going to be around the globe, rather than across the city or state. They will work in different time zones and cultures and speak different languages. The need to properly understand and evaluate these risks is increasing. On the legal front, financial institutions are required to map, measure, and assess specific risks related to money laundering and terror financing activities.

With the expansion of business and commercial activities around the world, financial crime has also increased. From commercial money laundering to embezzlement, from tax evasion to terror financing, there are people inside and outside of the organization who are actively looking for ways to capitalize on mistakes. When they find them, they act. Incidents of fraud, misuse of company information, money laundering, and other white collar crimes are all increasing.

In addition to geographic separation, AML programs now have to contend with a wide range of different regulatory environments, all throughout a single organization. Financial institutions today are likely to have differing language, cultural, and ethnic issues and diverse legal environments. These are all factors that impact the risk of potential money laundering and the likelihood that it will be found and resolved.

Language, Culture, and Ethnicity

A person's language, culture, and ethnicity are more than the way that person speaks, looks, and dresses. Language, culture, and ethnicity reflect core values, ideals, and ways of looking at the world. The structure of a language has a direct impact on the way a person thinks. One of the commonest blunders made by early explorers was failing to understand these differences. While people talk about the world shrinking, the reality is that it still contains a wide range of viewpoints and beliefs—factors that affect an employee's propensity to steal and willingness to cooperate with money launderers, terrorists, and tax evaders.

Understanding that there may be another viewpoint is half the battle. Allegations that involve a distant or international business location require an understanding that the risk profile has changed. It is not that one area is inherently more or less risky, based on the language or culture of the people. It is that when things change, they change. Differences large and small impact the potential risks, the implementation of programs, and the rationalizations made. No matter how politically correct the United States tries to be, the reality is that the rest of the world is not. Successful AML professionals have to work with the world as it is, not as it could be. The first step in confronting the risk of money laundering activities is a frank assessment of the situation, potential, and possibilities, no matter how difficult that may be to achieve.

For example, an AML professional who is fluent in a second language is not the same as a native speaker, though it is better than trying to manage a program through an interpreter. Knowing the cultural rules where the organization operates will not, in and of itself, make the AML program successful, but it does position the team to succeed. In addition to the language and cultural issues, there is also ethnicity. While there are a few racial groups and more language groups, there are even more ethnic groups. Most countries contain more than one ethnic group, and many contain dozens. Designing an AML program for Nigeria, with no understanding of the various linguistic, cultural, and ethnic issues in that country, would greatly limit the probability of success. Nigeria's borders, like many African countries, were created during the colonial period. As such, it contains several very different groups, primarily divided into the north and south. Each group has differing tribal, linguistic, and religious affiliations. Specific local knowledge is necessary to understand how the components will impact the money-laundering-related risks in that country. The same is true in other countries.

The Legal Landscape

Understanding the legal climate is important. All countries have legal processes for dealing with money laundering and terror financing. How you respond to these risks and what actions, mechanisms, and procedures are legal vary tremendously from region to region. Applying a standard operating procedure globally makes sense from an efficiency standpoint, but will embroil your procedures in a legal quagmire. There is no single standard level of proof or operating protocol that will be accepted globally. Instead, you will need to think outside of the box and focus on identifying the risks at a specific location and find locally effective means to mitigate those risks.

Criminal background checks are a part of many compliance programs, but the standards for these change radically across the globe. Many European countries restrict data to the individual concerned and law enforcement; there simply are no public records for convictions. To combat this, many organizations use third-party services, which have varying degrees of effectiveness. In Austria, as well as other European countries, criminal records are even purged from the state system after only a few years, meaning that a convicted money launderer could legitimately appear to have a clean record only a few years after being convicted.

Active investigations into individuals and organizations are illegal in parts of the Middle East and Asia, as well as certain tax havens and other locations. Most countries have specific prohibitions on how financial investigations are conducted (including the United States). In addition, any risk analysis must include extralegal considerations as well. Having a "foreigner" accuse a "local" can cause "difficulties" for companies operating in some countries. This can be especially problematic in small countries. Feeling "pushed around" can create a backlash that must be factored into the overall risk management model. After all, the goal is to achieve results from the AML program, not incite further abuses. On the positive side, getting government involvement, even at the highest levels, is often much easier in smaller countries (depending on the political implications). Understanding these elements can help guide the AML program specialists to make the best decision for the specific situation, rather than applying a cookie-cutter solution worldwide. This is not to imply that money laundering should be tolerated. But rather that there are many paths to the same destination, and alternative legal environments require finding alternative solutions that achieve the result within the law.

Geography: Distance Matters

Do not underestimate the power of distance. Even within the same country and region, isolated operations quickly develop localized "personalities" of their own. People working at remote locations, unpopular facilities, and other "unimportant" locations can have very different viewpoints from the corporate offices. Especially when you add the cultural and legal differences, geography can be a powerful force to deal with in managing these kinds of financial risks.

Psychologically, distance translates into independence of action. Many times, the first thing an AML professional hears upon landing at a distant office is some variation of "Dorothy, you are not in Kansas anymore." While this can be intimidating or even threatening, it can also be an asset. Since the rules are different, it means that all rules are different—both those that help and those that hinder—so a completely different approach is needed. Not only are the benefits of a familiar legal structure gone, but so are its limitations. Many times, this distance translates into flexibility that can work for you in resolving the issue in full compliance with the applicable standards.

Also remember that the interest and effectiveness of law enforcement and prosecutors vary across the range of legal systems. Working with a foreign company against local people is not popular anywhere. Be sure to identify local contributions made by your organization and emphasize the benefits of action.

The Goal of the Launderer Is to Hide

When people consider money laundering, the primary objective is ensuring that the laundering and underlying crime go undetected. Having discussed the U.S. model in more detail previously, comparison with the European model is in order. European AML policies and practices were established in 1991, when member countries harmonized their national laws and regulations to limit the ability of financial criminals to exploit the weaknesses in the financial systems. The next enhancement to the European AML regulations was issued in 2001 and, similar to the U.S. experience, was designed to strengthen the systems and extend the first line of defense. By focusing greater attention and penalties on narcotics trafficking and related financial misconduct, including tax evasion, the aim is to reprioritize both financial prevention and law enforcement objectives. A secondary objective was the extension of reporting responsibilities beyond the financial institution. It is worth noting just how significant this change is. For centuries, government was responsible for law enforcement. But AML laws began a transition. They placed responsibility for discovering and reporting lawbreakers on financial institutions. Now government policies are putting these responsibilities on others, to those who receive the funds, not just the financial institutions that process the funds. This expansion includes:

- Real estate agents
- External accountants, auditors, and consultants
- High-value auction houses
- Dealers in high value goods, such as precious stones or metals, or works of art
- Lawyers

At first glance this list looks obvious. Given further consideration, it really is a well-thought extension if the goal is to identify unusual transactions. Since financial institutions are already required to report, this points the spotlight of regulatory review right into the areas of greatest risk. It covers the categories of outside professionals who are most likely to be approached for assistance laundering funds, as well as the principal places one could convert cash to goods or vice versa.

The latest European Union expansion, in 2007, expanded the requirements in three specific higher-risk categories:

1. *Where there is no face-to-face communication with customers.* With globalization and technology, it is possible to initiate commercial relationships around the world. The kinds of business relationships that develop have a higher risk of potential abuse than a traditional business relationship.
2. *Connection to an overseas bank.* Due to the clear connection between international money flows and potential money laundering, customers with entirely domestic financial relationships would be at a lower risk than those with some connection to a foreign bank.
3. *People of position or political influence.* Where people have the potential to receive preferential treatment, greater care must be demonstrated to document that no such special consideration is provided in regard to potential money laundering or terror financing. While it is less likely that such persons engage in either activity directly, their status could be exploited by money launderers and terrorists.

The United States Takes a Different Approach

This path to compliance and early recognition of potential money laundering is different in the United States. With its strong focus on objective standards, the U.S. model relies on the creation and use of document reporting. While some of these standards have been expanded, they have only been expanded for currency transaction purposes and differ from the more complete list of reporting requirements issued by the European Union. The United States relies on two primary instruments:

1. Currency Transaction Report (CTR)
2. Suspicious Activity Report (SAR)

Of these, the CTR is now required to be filed by any business that transacts more than $10,000 in cash. The SAR is restricted to financial institutions, though it is mandated to be used by all types of regulated financial institutions, banks, securities houses, insurance companies, and money services businesses.

The value of these filings has grown rapidly due to inflation vis-à-vis the financial limit and the regulatory expansion of the reporting groups.

Since its inception in 1992, the SAR has been the most important tool in the U.S. model to reduce money laundering. The standard requires filing when an employee of a financial institution knows or has cause to suspect that a transaction may arise from illicit funds and be an illegal act and/or avoids the required reporting limits. When first introduced, SAR reporting was limited to banks, but that has been steadily expanded. Now there are over 23,000 reporting institutions, comprising banks, brokerages, insurance companies, casinos, and money services businesses. However, while the requirement has been expanded to nearly all financial firms, reporting volumes are dramatically weighted to traditional banking firms.

This is partly because of the definitions involved and the varying perspectives of the different types of financial institutions. Suspicious activity is defined to mean those actions that appear to have no business purpose, seem to violate some law, or could involve a bank employee in impropriety. Financial institutions are required to investigate indications of suspicious activity and report all instances that are not satisfactorily explained. The quest for uniform reporting with SARs is ongoing. Since the standard is suspicion, there is a bit of discretion that must be resolved by that individual institution. What is "suspicious" to one bank officer may not be "suspicious" to another.

Due in part to the sensitive nature of these investigations, and the difficulty in reporting customers to government agencies, the requirements also forbid notifying the customer of the suspicion or that the SAR has been filed. Aside from communications with authorized regulatory and law enforcement personnel, financial institutions are not allowed to admit that a specific SAR even exists.

Laundering Groups Seek to Evade Detection

Since most money laundering matters will involve that movement of funds across the globe, the discussion of regulatory differences is not merely an academic distinction but rather a snapshot of how the differing regulatory regimes will require differing actions on the part of the perpetrators. And since the relationship between terror financing and money laundering has clearly been established, some examples are appropriate.

Credit card fraud has been connected to terror financing for some time. In credit card fraud schemes, persons access legitimate credit card accounts to purchase resalable items or make direct cash advances. One scheme involved an Algerian group, connected to Al Qaeda, that was identified in 1997. The Algerians generated about $300,000 per year. Discovery came not through discovering the scheme, but when the Algerian group taught its scheme to other groups related to Al Qaeda operating in Afghanistan.

A few years later, another Algerian group also used a credit card scheme based on the theft of card details and signatures from two London pubs. The stolen data was taken to Belgium where duplicate cards were manufactured and encoded. The cards were used in vacation spots in France and Spain to minimize suspicion. The Algerians used the duplicate cards to generate resalable items and make direct cash withdrawals before selling the cards to still other persons to disguise their trail.

The proceeds from both Algerian schemes involved laundering funds through various banks in order to ultimately deposit them in Middle East banks.

A Fractured Enforcement and Regulatory Picture

The Algerian cases indicate that terror groups understand the controls in place and are adept at using technology, and that they educate each other about what they learn. This points to another area for collaboration as well as missed opportunity. Although the Office of the Comptroller of Currency (OCC), the Office of Thrift Supervision (OTS), the Federal Reserve (the Fed), and the Internal Revenue Service (IRS) play a role in AML efforts, it is the Drug Enforcement Agency (DEA), Customs Service, and the Federal Bureau of Investigation (FBI) as well as international law enforcement (such as MI5 and MI6 in the United Kingdom) that are on the front lines of combating money laundering, especially as criminal activities (drug trafficking, terror financing, and the like). The level of collaboration between regulators, regulated entities, and law enforcement personnel has a significant impact on the success of AML programs.

As the criminals adapt to technology with their *cyber laundering*, regulators and law enforcement personnel, too, must evolve. Regulators need to devise systems for faster access to cyber payment transaction systems and information. Guidance from the AML regulators and data discovered by AML audits can indicate exposures in various institutions and their rate of growth. As details of the cyber payment plan are an important program for money laundering and terror financing, these systems need greater transparency and accessibility of regulation and law enforcement agencies. Electronic commerce should be placed under the same supervision as brick-and-mortar banks.

The Regulatory Position on Cyber Risks

From the perspective of law enforcement supervision, cooperative financial institutions have to come into line with traditional money laundering guidelines by ensuring that program features in their cyber payment networks are in compliance. While the early focus was on the movement of cash in and out of financial institutions, it has now become apparent that electronic commerce will outpace cash, even for illicit payments, in the foreseeable future. So regulations will have to be reviewed to ensure they include cyber laundering activities. Government regulators and enforcement personnel must have access to these systems and data. For this to happen, the personnel of banks and other applicable institutions must be testing cyber financial systems for money laundering indicators, not just the traditional cash-based processes. The advantage to accepting digital currency is that it bypasses the controls around the cash area. Certain criminal groups have experimented with accepting payment by credit card, wire transfer, and other electronic payments for the past 15 years. In countries such as Japan and Australia, where cash is very uncommon in everyday usage, the percentage of illicit funds paid electronically has grown dramatically.

Internet banking services facilitate cyber laundering. They enable global money movement with minimal review. Non-financial institutions also process online payments. The oldest is PayPal. As a conduit for processing online payments, the company connects persons engaged in business transactions. For moving money, these services can be used to avoid certain controls. PayPal structures its operations to ensure that its customers remain under the reporting lines. Because accounts are typically capped at $10,000 per month in activity, it is unlikely that a large-scale money laundering operation would use PayPal. However, there are other payment processing entities located around the globe. Some are more reputable than others. Some companies, however, locate to offshore havens or micronations where they can effectively be free of enforceable regulation.

Guidelines that discuss cyber payments and recommend efforts to reduce cyber laundering encounter two major issues. First, there are no standardized global systems for the supervision and coordination of all cyber payments. This lack of a system can be addressed through an extension of the Financial Action Task Force (FATF) guidelines. Indeed, such a system may emerge from other forums, but its main function should be to monitor, to provide regulations, to provide law enforcement, and to provide auditing. The second is the legal framework within which these cyber payment entities operate. While some would argue that cyber payments should be restricted to authorized financial institutions, the technology has already outpaced those entities. Absent some global government, there is no practical way to stop some nonfinancial entity for setting up a payment processing service.

Simple Fraud, Still Successful

One of the best illustrations of the challenges faced by regulators and AML teams can be summed up in the classic 419 fraud scheme. These schemes take their name from the Nigerian Criminal Code that makes them illegal.

419 schemes constitute one of the most basic and well-documented type of fraud schemes. They thrive because the perpetrators have adapted to evolving technology, changing regulatory requirements, and enhanced law enforcement pressure. They succeed in laundering illicit proceeds through banks and other financial institutions worldwide.

The scheme involves an unsolicited letter from a foreign individual (usually in a developing nation) who claims to have access to some large fund that he needs help in transferring out of the country by either legitimate or illegitimate means. These letters are very often from Nigeria. They are sent using commercially available e-mail, fax, and snail mail lists to thousands of recipients. (Many are in the United States, where such letters have a reputation.)

The gist of the letters, no matter what country the particular letter purportedly emanates from, is that the writers need a receiver's cooperation to access certain funds. The letter writers will pay the receiver a substantial fee for helping them. In some cases, they ask the receiver to create an invoice; in others, they simply ask for the wiring details for where to deposit money into a receiver's account. Some letters require that the receiver travel to a particular country to access the funds, possibly setting the stage for a kidnapping incident.

The following is the unedited text of one letter.

dear sir,

<u>appeal for urgent assistance</u>

i know this letter may come to you as surprise, but it has come to a matter i can no longer help hence my appeal for assistance

meanwhile, to be brief, i am the wife of late general sanni aba-cha the former head of the state of nigeria who died on the 8th june, 1998 under mysterious circumstances

following the death of my husband a lot of things has gone wrong within my family. virtually all member of my family are under house arrest.

most importantly, my husbands accounts all over the owrld has been frozened by the present administration, the most recent is <u>£3.6 billion pound sterling in a london account, N2.2 billion in a nigerian account and a lot of others to mention but a few.</u>

it is under this circumstance that i plead with you to liase with mr. david eze an attorney at law who has been our personal advise for over 20 years: arrange and meet with him and dis-cuss the most possible way to withdraw for safekeeping with youthe sum of <u>US$98.5M (ninety eight million, five hundred thousand united states dollars).</u>

this amount was deposited in a coded account with a security company in one of the west african countries. you should feel free to negotiate all other terms with the <u>gentleman david eze esq</u> as you can reach him on <u>telefax 234-1-4924158.</u>

but because of the high level of secrecy and confidentiality required for the success of the transaction we require you to use this transaction code ma-de/98 in all correspondeces.

i wish only you should understand the need for face to face meeting as this is the only hope of the entire family. we do hope and appreciate that should this fund be deposited with you for mnagement with the wealth of your experience. we will be rest assured that any time we are released from detention we shall have some things to fall back on.

finally, we plead that should you be in a position to assist. we pray that you keep it sealed as the next party does not need to hear about it for security reason

we look forward to your kind co-operation

These letters are uniformly directed to senior executives, business owners, and others who fall into certain profiles. The groups that sponsor them are all based in countries that have legal systems with limited ability to control or punish the perpetrators. As the above letter indicates, they play to the sense of adventure and greed in the recipient, evoking images of Humphrey Bogart in *Casablanca*, where great rewards are possible to people of action. In fact, there are no such funds, and if the appeal were made for a few thousand dollars the letter would be instantly discarded. But when the stakes are raised, there is a certain percentage of the population that will become involved in these schemes. Interestingly, it is typically educated and successful businesspeople who fall prey to these schemes, sometime even dragging their companies into the resulting mess.

This scheme depends on a variety of factors and each letter is styled to accentuate these key points, masking the obvious deficiencies behind the request with pleas for secrecy, secret codes, and large sums. The net effect is that the victim has to actively take part in the perpetration of the scheme, up to and including international travel, the establishment of foreign bank accounts, and other such active mechanisms. The frantic pace set by the letter writer ensures that each of the respondents acts quickly and in secrecy, thus limiting the amount of objective counsel and scrutiny that is sought.

The final key is the introduction of paranoia and greed into the transaction. "Hurry," "They are trying to stop us," "If we don't act quickly, the funds will be gone," and like prompts are designed to encourage the victim's participation and limit the likelihood of telling others about the scheme. This is so successful that many victims refuse to report the crime, even after they have been taken, and others refuse to cooperate with authorities because of their perceived participation and gullibility.

The scheme's perpetrators focus on specific target groups and the psychology of mass marketing to establish their scheme. They send varied mailings to people throughout the developed nations based around profiles and industry groups. Highly visible people are likely to be targeted, as are entrepreneurs, senior managers, and small-business owners. The second level of the scheme is often more subtle in that they often ask the victims to refer others in the course of the scheme, thus further making the victim into an active participant.

The scheme resolves in one of two outcomes. Either the victim has gotten off the hook in the process, or they have been relieved of their bank balances. In the case of corporate involvement, businesses have found entire operating and benefits accounts cleaned out by international wire, with the funds rapidly moved across the globe. In the above letter, the groundwork is clearly being laid to demand the respondent travel to Nigeria to consummate the deal. This will probably lead to the respondent's kidnapping, as the resulting ransom demand is much simpler for the fraudster to pursue.

Conclusion

While it would seem that these schemes are amazingly transparent, there are a number of intelligent and experienced business people who are taken in by them every year. In some notable instances, this has involved the use of corporate proceeds at substantial organizations. The relevance for AML professions is that these schemes lure, entice, and encourage people to actively take part in a fraud scheme, set up and participate in the laundering of the illicit proceeds, and commit other financial crimes. In many cases, the recipient becomes a victim, as his information is used to launder the funds out of his or his company's bank account. Where this kind of obvious scheme can turn ordinary people into money launderers, the lesson for AML professionals is clear—much has to be done to address the opportunity risks in the current financial institution model.

This new generation of money launderers has diversified their approach to take advantage of the speed and security that technology provides. They have adapted to nonbank financial firms and even nonfinancial exchange services to move funds globally. These technologies, and the real economic value of having large sums flowing through a nation's economy, show the level of innovation that is confronting traditional AML controls. This could constitute a "privatization" of money laundering methods, by moving the fund transfer mechanism out of the government regulated banks and into more anonymous entities.

CHAPTER 9

Investigating Money Movement

Money Laundering Is Now Transnational Organized Crime

In 2002, the United Nations sponsored the Palermo Convention on Transnational Organized Crime, resulting in an agreement signed by 184 countries. This framework establishes international cooperation in fighting organized crime and addresses money laundering and terror financing.

Palermo built upon the first and second Basel Accords. A third Basel meeting is thought to be in the works. The original Basel participants were the central banks of Belgium, Canada, France, Germany, Italy, Japan, Luxembourg, the Netherlands, Spain, Sweden, Switzerland, United Kingdom, and the United States. Basel I and Basel II set the stage for most of the anti-money-laundering (AML) provisions in place today.

Building on this foundation, legal and regulatory requirements have made specific chargeable acts within the illicit movement of funds. These have not been universally accepted. In the United States, efforts to require financial institutions to confirm the source of customer funds met great resistance. Banks, specifically, felt that they were going to be held accountable for the criminal acts of others. After much debate, the final requirement was for enhanced know-your-customer rules, requiring verification of the individual's identity by an official government issued identity document and retention of documents used in opening accounts.

Succeeding in the Investigative Process

Success in money laundering investigations is not due to a single source. It entails assembling sufficient data to show that a given transaction is a sham. Sometimes that takes extensive effort; other times it is merely a matter of confirming the source of recipient of funds. What makes the process difficult is not the information needed. It is the lack of a central source for the relevant data and the differing access that employees, regulators, and law enforcement each has. Data sources to consider include:

- *Documents captured via search warrant.* Since money laundering cases often result from underlying criminal cases, the existing investigative file may have substantial corroborative evidence. Where the investigation begins with the laundering aspects, it is common to subpoena documents including financial records, brokerage statements, property records, telephone records, open loans, and so on.
- *Law enforcement databases include mineable data.* For example, after criminal history and conviction records, the Financial Crimes Enforcement Network (FinCEN) records include Suspicious Activity Reports (SAR), Currency Transaction Reports (CTR), Currency or Monetary Instrument Report (CMIR), and so forth, by name and can be searched for matching names, details, locations, or even patterns.
- *Database records from the financial sector.* For example, documents and loan accounts, past account history, related parties, and so forth.
- *Court filings.* Including criminal, civil, and bankruptcy records for the people and business entities involved.
- *Other public records.* Including automobile ownership, wedding licenses, official permits, and press articles.

Analysis of the data is designed to identify inconsistencies. Analytical proof, rather than direct proof, is an assessment of the reasonableness of state financial activities. The most common of these accounting tools are the comparative net worth analysis, income and expense comparison, and bank deposit analysis. These tools compare the claimed activity with the visible records and evaluate the relative value of the missing data, if any.

Government Access to Information

Since the early 1990s, the problem has not been the analysis of the data; it has been access to data. This began inside and outside of the financial system. With the advent of Internet-based banking, protection and verification of the data was paramount. The U.S. government proposed using the Clipper chip, an 80-bit encryption, as a key component of the program, with one aspect being that the government would have access to decrypt the data if it needed it. The response was overwhelmingly negative from the public and the banking sector. Many viewed government access as an illegal search. In response, Internet banking evolved slowly as people were not comfortable with the safety of their data. It illustrated that the government was interested in looking at financial data and, counterproductively, spurred the growth of privacy-oriented software development that advertised products that prevented government observation. For example, PGP (pretty good privacy) began showing up on criminals' computers, encoding the illicit data and making retrieval for evidentiary purposes much more difficult.

Today, most online banking uses the secure and trusted Transport Layer Security (TLS) protocols. These do not allow a government "back door," so online banking payments may undergo less scrutiny from an AML perspective.

This brief history provides the foundation for the data access challenge that cyber payment programs provide. Several competing cyber currency plans are in development and in various stages of use globally, though there are two leading concepts. The first builds off of the public confidence in credit cards and expands on that model—the smart card. The other is the creation of truly virtual currencies or "electronic cash." The ideas that support these two technologies have begun to converge so that cyber payments represent a large infrastructure.

So how does this history and trend in the privacy of records impact the narcotics trade? There is no doubt that the only reason the drug trade exists is for the money. The risks, penalties, and survival rate would never be tolerated but for the money. So protecting the money, mitigating the risks, and limiting the odds of prosecution all become valid objectives. It is well known that efforts to combat illicit narcotics are intertwined with illicit cash.

Since the output of methamphetamine (a manufactured drug), along with cannabis, heroin, and cocaine smuggling (natural drugs), are often sold via the same channels, it is unrealistic to try to effectively differentiate the types of drugs from the drug money. In trying to reduce the flow of illegal drugs, law enforcement uses the data from money flow patterns and sales distribution data to identify the distribution networks and attack at multiple levels. By disrupting the supply, distribution, and sales channels in tandem, law enforcement can damage the organizations or disband them. But if the criminal organization's data is protected and the supply chain cannot be identified, then it will simply restock and begin again. Law enforcement has extensive experience with the hydra-headed structure of these organizations down to the lowest sales level. By coordinating the financial investigation, not only will the supply be disrupted, but the means to pay for resupply will be removed.

Mining Data for Money Laundering

The Bank Secrecy Act (BSA) set the precedent of later statutes that focus on the structure of the transaction itself and not the individual criminal offenses. In this way, the laundering transaction must be proven to result from or involve some underlying criminal act. Even terror financing is tied to an underlying act: the support of the terror organization. For these reasons, in order to prosecute access to the underlying data or an alternative method of proof, is required.

With the advent of FinCEN reporting in 1990, mineable databases provided another means of proof. Obviously, if the person is caught in the act, that evidence is appropriate. But typically the people caught are lower-level participants and, in the effort to convict the leaders, access to more data is required.

Suspicious activity reports (SAR) arrived with the 1992 update, providing a much broader range of data in the FinCEN archives. This can help expand the understanding of the banking acts and even possible relationships. Since the standard is only suspicious behavior, however, this is a double-edged sword. The lower standard generates more possible data, but the depth of data is limited.

So the changing technology, with the increasing regulatory pressure, comes together to provides commercial implications and exposures in cyber payment measures. As current models deploy, they provide secure, confidential, anonymous payment transfer mechanisms for payer and recipient—which makes international purchases highly attractive to money laundering.

In considering the field of cyber payment AML, it should be recorded as data inherent. Cyber payment goods can be accumulated in trackable and traceable systems. But the current trend does not require that evolutionary path. Fears of increased government surveillance of data are often considered an invasion of privacy. Proper regulation and deterrence of money laundering and terror financing, however, require active inspection of these transactions.

Some Products Help the Perpetrators

The impact of privacy objectives, from both legitimate and criminal sectors, can be seen in the evolution of mobile telephone services. Initially these services were modeled on home telephone services, where customers have a single account. Charges were credit based and thus required detailed customer data, which resulted in extensive administrative and back-office expenses. In responding to customer concerns over excess charges, the industry proposed a prepaid telephone option. The lower cost of handsets facilitated this, too, because the real economic value was in the provision of services. With prepaid plans, the service fees are collected in advance, negating the need for billing and collection expenses and reducing the administrative and back-office expenses.

Prepaid cell phones became extremely popular among criminals because they allow them to communicate with anonymity. It is simply cost effective for narcotic dealers to replace their handsets on a periodic basis. (Also, by using standard telephone service subscriptions and restricting criminal activities to prepaid phones, criminals reduce the odds of discovery and provable criminal conduct.)

Given the experience of prepaid mobile telephones, other technologies will follow similar patterns of criminal exploitation and used for money laundering and terrorism. These technologies include smart-chip-encoded phones, smart cards, e-money, and other digital forms of currency.

Investigating Virtual Payment Technologies

The primary player in a virtual wallet program is PayPal. Owned by eBay, PayPal is a payment facilitation plan for online transactions between individuals and businesses. PayPal is the largest successful example of a nonfinancial technology company that facilitates digital currency transfers.

PayPal is hardly alone. Platforms that use smart-chip-enabled cards, mobile telephones, and other devices are being designed and tested. These include payroll-oriented labor cards, reloadable and exchangeable cards, and other variations. The key element is that while these technologies replace older forms of manual payment, they do not come with the same kinds of controls. For example, social benefits (welfare, aid programs, refunds, and other financial assistance from governmental and NGO sources) are provided on the lowest level of these devices—reloadable debit cards. The card is issued to the beneficiary, and then it is reloaded remotely on a periodic basis. But there is no way of determining who has access and control of the card. Moving up in complexity, the use of virtual wallet technologies, like PayPal, enables the sharing of login and password data, effectively granting access to an account to anyone, anonymously.

With smart-chip-equipped devices, the opportunities expand dramatically. A preloaded device can be used to pay for subway fare, a newspaper, and a cup of coffee. Seen as a cash replacement, it can also be used to pay for illicit services. When coupled with a receiving device, a person can use a smart-chip-enabled telephone to text funds from one device to another. Many narcotics arrests are made on the basis of watching the exchange of cash. What will the probable cause be when all that is seen is a person texting another?

The key to the common usage of these technologies is the ability to both send and receive. That is why PayPal is so popular; it can be used to purchase or sell with two-way access to funds. The smart card can store data from a central server and allow nonaligned anonymous transactions, too. Smart cards can be purchased to keep the value, and with cards that contain 80 times more data than traditional cards. Numerous companies and joint ventures are developing platforms for smart cards. These platforms are far more advanced in Australia and Japan, where they are more common than in Europe or the United States, where they are still in preliminary testing.

Another platform is the memory card, functioning more as a reloadable alternative to a traditional credit card or debit card. These cards use the same validation systems and thus create traditional paper trails. The appeal of the smart cards is the lack of a required trail through any financial institutions. Currently, memory cards require sufficient control to avoid using them for money laundering.

Another variation is online escrow sites, such as escrow. com, auctionchex.com, docdata.com, and iloxx.de, which hold funds for parties until both sides agree on the amount of the transaction. These are marketed as "consumer-to-consumer contracts," with buyers and sellers setting the conditions online. Upon joint agreement, the escrow service funds the transaction. This relieves the unknowns of dealing with individual level sales, in that the buyer knows the funds are safe until the conditions are met, and the seller knows that the buyer is able to close the deal with good funds. At this point, the safety and security of the systems seem quite high, assuming the integrity of the escrow service itself.

Related services use telephone-based billing to accomplish similar outcomes. The most prominent is the eCharge phone, which is a worldwide network of 800/900 premium rate billing telephone numbers. eCharge now processes virtual credit cards, debit cards, and stored value, allowing customers to make payments without any personal financial information being part of the transaction.

Looking to the Future Investigative Issues

A rapidly expanding and innovative series of transaction methodologies has developed that do not run through traditional financial institutions and are not currently subject to financial institution regulation. That does not make them criminal, but like the prepaid telephone discussed in the previous section, they can be highly exploitable by money launderers.

Network-based electronic payment and smart-card-based systems can facilitate money laundering and provide alternatives to banking services. Opportunities have been identified by money launderers who use cyber payment processes without alerting the various cyber payment networks' abuse programs. These demonstrations will help set the direction and guidelines that can reduce cyber laundering.

Moving to actual digital currencies yields increased risks for laundering money. All digital currency sites have the same risk profiles in that they purport to offer anonymous electronic payments processing, which is perfect for people buying and selling illicit items. These include actual payment and storage sites, online casinos, and even virtual online games—including sites that offer digital gold currency such as e-gold Ltd., which was discussed in Chapter 5.

Online casinos market themselves as gambling venues; however, they actually function as anonymous financial account holders. Although these systems purport to exist for recreational reasons, they also provide a way to launder money quickly. These transactions are almost instantaneous and can be done from home.

The vastly increasing speed of these transactions and the shift from bank- to online-based transactions have effectively made seizing the proceeds difficult. In the e-gold Ltd. case, even though it was located outside of the United States, its operators were within the United States, allowing for effective prosecution.

Drug users, in contrast to drug sellers, will typically use these technologies for one-time purchases. The card can then be taken to a merchant or machine where additional funds can be loaded on the card. Furthermore, the funds can be transferred from a bank account or other card type to the smart card. For the seller, when the card reaches a predetermined level, it can be used to fund domestic or offshore accounts as needed. Cards can be amassed so that more substantial sums can be collected before the card balances are transferred. This is the equivalent of collecting cash, but without the resulting risk or suspicion. As smart cards become common, the devices to load and unload the smart cards will as well. When smart chips are installed in telephones, the data on the smart chip can be unloaded via text message to the receiving bank account. Such capacities support the claim that these new technologies can circumvent existing AML controls.

If the smart card is recovered, it is possible that it might retain some history of the activity. High-value smart cards can be modified so that they capture details of the financial transactions. While these details remain anonymous, they can allow for the tracking of the movement of individual transactions as they aggregate. And in contrast to cash, smart cards are small, light, innocuous-looking devices that are highly efficient for trafficking currency. Assuming that the criminal obtains what will soon be readily available transfer equipment, these tools will provide fast and efficient transfer of illicit funds to consolidation accounts. Once the capital is comingled into the nonfinancial system, it is not realistic to distinguish legitimate funds from illicit payments.

And smart cards have the ability to move funds onto other devices. By loading the card into a personal computer or even a smart-card-equipped phone, the funds can be transferred via the Internet to any Web-based financial system. The sheer variety of options, when funds are freed from the traditional banking system, will radically reshape money laundering controls from the way they are practiced today.

In the skilled use of the Internet, the latest trend is the trouble. Usually small transactions will not be monitored even in the most carefully controlled banking systems. Bear in mind these are deposits, not withdrawals. They create no liability for the institution, aside from regulatory compliance. So the incentive to screen them is under threat since they are not in the economic self-interest of the institution. Since these smaller value deposits are less likely to generate suspicion, they can also be used to model a structuring operation, with numerous low value deposits being added to traditional banking accounts. But more realistically, these proceeds will remain safely on stored-value cards rather than ever hitting the traditional banking sector at all. Where would be the benefit to the money launderer, who has gone to such effort to avoid attention, to deliberately risk discovery by depositing directly to domestic accounts when he can just as easily deposit to international accounts?

Putting an Investigative Plan in Motion

With the foundation prepared, the next step is to develop an investigative plan to address potential financial crimes. Any investigation into money laundering, terror financing, or other financial crimes must begin by looking at three potential perpetrator markers: (1) their behavior (what they like to do), (2) their finances (what they can afford to do), and (3) their business (the financial vehicles they have access to). When reviewing

169

financial accounts, look for the following indicators for potential money laundering:

- Significant or excessive cash
- Unexplained or unusual cash disbursements
- Withdrawals or cash payments that match cash transactions by the suspect
- Cash deposits or expenditures
- Visits to safe deposit boxes
- Purchases of traveler's or cashier's checks
- Excessive use of private mail deliveries

The investigator must remember that the trail will be disguised—concealed by both misdirection and deliberate acts of deception. As such, nothing is more important than the continual verification of information, including validation of all documents, shredding statements, and vetting all witnesses. Remember to question everything, assuming that it can be falsified. The investigation itself is built on this continually questioning methodology and requires access to personal and business financial records to successfully identify the money laundering and, most important, the true beneficiaries of the scheme.

People Are Essential to Proof

Identify people who have the information necessary to prove, disprove, or validate both statements and documentation. Former employees, confidants, and spouses can be tremendous sources of information. Compile the available records on the people and entities, beginning on the outside; these include public records, private records, and others. These records provide great detail on the money launderer, and the associated parties, but bear in mind nearly all these documents come from the subject directly, meaning that their veracity must be questioned. Just because the document is housed in a government office does not make it accurate.

After the records have been analyzed and all useful information extracted, prepare for the subject interview. Cover the basics, including history, pedigree, family connections, and other ancillary data that either explains sources of funds or precludes the subject from raising them later. Carefully walking through each area may be painstaking, but it is essential. Specifically pin the subject down on bank names, accounts, access, and connections. Drill down to specifics regarding sources, income, loans, and any unusual financial dealings. Look for indicators of falsified business dealings, including:

- "Consulting" fees or commissions
- Payments to middlemen, agents, or brokers
- Payments to subcontractors
- Inflated or unusual payments to regular suppliers
- Payments to ghost employees
- Inflated draws by owners of the paying business
- Payments from "off-book" slush funds, affiliates, or subsidiaries

Putting these investigative tools into action provides insight into the illicit activities disguised in seemingly ordinary business activities. When faced with schemes that involve collusion between employees and outside fraudsters, these tools become essential, as shown in the following case study regarding the risk from your organization's employees and contractors working abroad. These employees are often empowered far beyond corresponding domestic positions, and there are many barriers to thorough oversight.

Finding Money Laundering Abroad

A U.S.-based financial institution has operating units in several South and Central American countries. During a standard review of one of the South American units, the auditors discovered a number of unreconciled accounts. This was claimed to be an accounting error, as the income and balance statements were in line and the unit was reporting a profit each period. However, after several weeks, the team was able to reconcile several areas, with the exception of the foreign exchange area. Their analysis revealed substantial shortages in the foreign currency cash accounts. The records also indicated an extensive network of foreign currency trading customers, most with unusual or incomplete account information. Looking deeper into the relationship between the manger for that area and the customers, they discovered a correlation between the foreign exchange transactions and payments to his family members through their personal accounts.

Upon discovery, a number of employees came forward, telling management about his activities and their concerns. Several admitted to having been involved in the scheme, including getting some small benefits, though the manager received the majority of the benefit. They gave statements that recounted how he had ordered the staff to comply with his instructions regarding these customers or lose their jobs. Since the region was economically depressed, they had no recourse but to comply. Through his various schemes the controller laundered over $16 million through the institution's accounts.

All companies are vulnerable to this type of fraud. Perhaps not in the same way, or via that same scheme, but every organization has a weakness that a senior insider can abuse. Typically, this type of scheme affects larger companies, especially those with operational units in emerging regions. These companies rely on a network of professionals to manage their operations, develop business, and identify sustainable markets in diverse conditions. Under these circumstances, it is easier for controls to fail and for policies and procedures to be violated without notice.

While the proper controls are theoretically in place, there are several key controls that are weakened, at least to some extent, in the international arena. The first cause for this is simple geography. The further people are apart, the more difficult it is to properly guard against dishonesty. Factoring in the complication of cultural, legal, and language differences, the chances for successful dishonesty increase dramatically.

The next complication is in the strength of external controls. Each country has varying degrees of effectiveness for legal and law enforcement actions. Even external auditing standards vary tremendously. As this company learned (and Enron subsequently demonstrated), having an international accounting firm audit the books provided no real protection because annual audits failed to identify any of the irregularities or money laundering. In this case, the company initiated litigation against the auditors, alleging that a proper audit would have discovered the illicit activities. The subsequent review of the auditors' work papers identified numerous areas where they had not even tested the numbers and schedules provided. In other instances, they signed off on documents that never existed. Companies that rely on external audits of international locations will find that the actual level of protection can often be less than perceived. Audits are not intended to find dishonesty and depend on the integrity of management to evaluate the financial results.

Money Laundering Exposure during the Financial Industry Consolidation

Dramatic growth followed by the sudden contraction of the global economy has led to the consolidation of many financial institutions. Either through the collapse of the institution or economic necessity to avoid collapse, the merger and acquisition process presents some unique challenges for AML teams.

With financial industry companies racing to join the crowd with larger and more aggressive mergers, it is simply a matter of time before some missed opportunities occur. As it happens, there have now been several mergers, including both vertical and horizontal integration efforts where the benefits were never realized, and the costs make the whole effort appear to be a waste of management time. Recent reports in the *Wall Street Journal* as well as other business periodicals detail an astoundingly high rate of failures in high-profile combinations. Finally, shareholders are starting to question the realization of value from this tremendous commitment of management time and corporate resources.

Change is the single best enabler of fraud schemes. By altering the traditional processes and procedures, companies create opportunity for a dishonest person to successfully affect a scheme. In the flurry of merger and acquisition (M&A) activity, companies are radically and rapidly restructuring whole operational processes in their effort to consolidate functional responsibilities. It is this quest for operational efficiencies through growth, merger, and acquisition that creates these opportunities. Management and control functions are simply overwhelmed by the pace and rate of change, leaving holes in the company's armor.

To enable these integrations, many merger scenarios include the divestiture of certain units. Either to accommodate certain anticompetition requirements or to streamline among core competencies, these strategic divestitures create identical opportunities for change-based fraud schemes on the M&A side of the equation. In fact, companies are often much less concerned about the operational performance of a unit that is being spun off, even to the extent of dumping poor performers and problem issues into the unit prior to letting it go. While this may seem an expedient method of getting rid of your problems, it will create enhanced opportunity for schemes, including money laundering to go undetected. Should the divestiture fail or be cancelled, the company could end up with Frankenstein's monster.

While it is impossible to stop motivated and dishonest people from targeting your company, there are steps that you can take to limit your risk of acquiring these problems in the course of a merger or acquisition. The key is in the makeup and intent of the due diligence process. For many companies, due diligence efforts are limited to key operations management personnel assisted by limited audit and legal resources. These efforts are usually inadequate to protect the company's interests from deliberate schemes or uncover indications of money laundering. The due diligence process should be a team-based review that analyzes all aspects of the proposed venture, including all negative ramifications.

As such, the internal auditor should be looking for compliance with current control procedures. Lawyers should be looking at known and anticipated liabilities. (Who really wants to acquire large known liabilities in this litigious culture?) Operations management should be looking at ease of integration and potential synergies. Investigators should be looking for unanticipated problems, including both deliberate and systematic issues. Too often the modern due diligence exercise consists of a hasty verification of known information, rather than a detailed review of the situation. By adding investigative due diligence, companies can mitigate risks on the front end.

Despite the seemingly obvious risks inherent in M&A activity, the key similarities for when crime cases arise are abuse of controls that have been abandoned or overwhelmed in the quickly changing atmosphere. Every money laundering scheme is customized to the organization and the opportunities available to the criminal. In preparing to evaluate potential vulnerability, the investigator should be prepared to conduct a "what-if" analysis to determine the reasonably possible actions by each potential player and establish whether or not proper controls are in place.

Similarly, if your organization is undergoing even small amounts of M&A activity, analyzing the due diligence areas in the process will forewarn the investigators. Incorporation of these risk mitigation techniques can help minimize money laundering opportunities. Practically, however, all M&A activity involves turmoil, and instances where these kinds of financial misconduct opportunities can arise if left unchecked.

The most common type of change-based misconduct is from employees. These may be people who are disillusioned by the process or believe that they are slated for reduction. The stresses of the transition may push them past their ordinary boundaries. Whatever the cause, these internal disaffected persons pose the greatest risk to the company.

While some schemes are committed by one person, it is difficult for one person, no matter what position they are in, to perpetrate a complex scheme by themselves. But a combination of persons, acting in concert, can damage any organization if they are properly positioned. To properly assess the risk factor for employee involvement in money laundering schemes, the potential combinations of people and positions must be analyzed for early-warning signs.

Unfortunately, in many organizations, management is often predisposed to find fault or expect problems with lower-level employees and, equally, to not see problems with upper-level or executive employees. AML practices should focus on identifying the potential abuses in a given position and ensuring that proactive protections are in place, especially with regards to senior-level positions. This is especially true in M&A activities, where midlevel and senior managers are vital to the transition process.

Investigators can position themselves to effectively anticipate, control, and manage the risk of potential liability by appre-
ciating the full extent of the damage that can be done by the
dishonest employee, damage that escalates according to the
level of the employee. In planning for these contingencies and
preparing preventive measures, the company must account for
the financial exposure, the possible participation of one or more
executives, and the loss of business activity stemming from the
efforts devoted to discovery and investigation.

Conclusion

While many people still perceive money laundering as exotic
and unlikely to occur, AML professionals know better. An increasing number of companies are discovering that they have
become involved in these schemes, even nonfinancial firms, because management is not expected to pay as close attention
when a company is at one of these key transition points. The
attacks are focused and structured with specific objectives. And
unfortunately many of them are never discovered.

What is important in implementing preventive planning or
handling fraud cases is that these people strike from the inside
at the vulnerable areas in your organization. By identifying those
particular areas where controls are either not in place or ineffective, the dishonest employee begins to conceive a specific
plan. "20/20 hindsight" is a phrase that is often used in discussing these cases. Once uncovered, the scheme becomes so
apparent that people often wonder how it was possible that no
one caught on. However, it is important to remember that the
key to a successful fraud is that honest persons should not suspect. Employee schemes and espionage cases alike depend on
this failure of the control process.

CHAPTER 10

Reporting and Recovery

Reporting to Law Enforcement

Various reporting mechanisms are tied to specific enforcement actions and serve multiple roles for discovering laundered funds and prosecuting money launderers. The Currency and Monetary Instrument Report (CIMR) is often used at border crossings, which covers the transportation of cash or negotiable instruments of greater than $10,000. There is nothing illegal about transporting large volumes of cash or negotiable instruments, but the reporting requirements confuse criminals.

How reporting mechanisms are used can be seen at border crossings nearly every day. For example, an individual in Juarez, Mexico, sought to test the system and see how carefully currency inspections were being conducted by bringing U.S. currency back into the country. He carefully packaged $170,000 and instructed one of his employees to carry a currency bag with $20,000 in it. Upon arriving at the border, the carrier completed the CIMR for $20,000. Based on his responses, he was selected for screening and asked the destination of the funds. He stated that the $20,000 was going to a nearby Texas bank. When he was asked if that was all the money going to the bank, he asked to revise his form because "in error" he had recorded the wrong amount. When he pulled out the additional $170,000 it was seized by the border agents based on his having only put

179

$20,000 on the CIMR. The government prosecuted the case against the contraband funds and the defendant appealed, losing at the 5th Circuit Court of Appeals.

Money laundering cases require overwhelming evidence of the scheme or, like tax evasion cases, clear instances where incorrect information was recorded on the forms. In the previous example, the $190,000 clearly looked like an attempt to smuggle money into the country. It is unlikely that the border crossing agent or courts would have ruled the same way if the amount unrecorded was $5.

Though seemingly harsh, the purpose of the recording forms is to force the individuals to declare a position. For a variety of reasons, lawful people tend to declare their positions honestly and criminals tend to declare their positions dishonestly. Again, given the previous example, had the courier declared $190,000, he may or may not have been allowed into the country. But he would have kept his currency had he not filed a grossly inaccurate form.

Honest People Act Differently

There are other examples of people searched by the police and found to be possessing large amounts of cash. The cash may or may not have originated from a lawful purpose. The distinguishing event takes place when the law enforcement officer asks if the cash belongs to the bearer. If the bearer establishes ownership over the cash, there is no crime, assuming that he is not crossing the border (or has filed the appropriate paperwork when crossing the border). A large percentage of people, however, will not claim ownership of the cash, believing that it is "less guilty" to do so.

When a law enforcement officer finds a large amount of unclaimed cash, he is required to seize it until the legitimate

180

owner claims it. This is a very important aspect of the documentation process. Money launderers will lie in the process; they cannot tell the truth about the source of the proceeds. So if the transaction is set up in such a fashion that they decide to lie, then the falsification can be grounds for seizure, as in the example earlier.

Working backward through the various legislation, the pattern is clear. The penalties for specific violations are increasing for financial institutions that allow, enable, and accept money laundering activities and the individuals who attempt to get away with these activities. Financial crimes can entail prison sentences, but the weight of the punishment is deprivation of ill-gotten gains. A review of U.S. Federal Court filings will reveal a long and steadily growing list of cases filed against the amounts of currency. While these seizures cannot compensate for the harm done by the criminal acts and the costs of defending against them, they can help to balance the scales by making the costs of laundering more expensive and deter persons from attempting to abuse the U.S. financial system.

There are two aspects of the existing legislation that provide enforcement guidance for cyber laundering. The first aspect involves the value and cost of the equipment necessary to conduct these schemes; the second is the high probability that criminal cyber payments involve the use of funds actually deposited in traditional financial institution accounts. Once the funds are comingled, the entire account can be subject to seizure.

Anticipating Challenges with Cyber Recoveries

Recoveries from cyber laundering will become increasingly difficult as the movement of funds speeds up in response to the perceived risk of seizure. Advanced data mining procedures will help to indentify patterns of abuse, but the search technologies confront huge increases in volume and growth of alternative payment processors. Thus, the net impact of these changes will become apparent only over time.

To date, the various issuing entities involved in cyber cash, smart cards, reloadable traditional cards, and related technologies have kept payment limits relatively low. Compared to credit cards, that can mean tens of thousands of dollars, and many of the test products have limits capped at $500. One test of organizational commitment to anti-money laundering (AML) will be where the issuers set the limits for these products. However, the issuers could argue that the market will establish its own comfort points. However, it seems likely that the need for high-value alternative payment and financial storage devices is overwhelmingly in the criminal classes.

Possible other regulatory tools would include mandating a cap on these nonfinancial system products. This can be difficult to implement. Regulatory agencies would do well to recall the Clipper chip episode, where pushing a technology beneficial to the government drove law-abiding people to the opposite product mix. Similarly, regulators could impose a total volume cap on these cards, allowing them to have a longer life cycle, but capping them from being used repeatedly for high-value transactions. Under this scenario, the card might be capped at three times the initial funding. Again, this has potential challenges because the forced limitations may drive more people toward products that are perceived to be less restrictive.

Other options include trying to restrict the licensing of the software and hardware used to reload these devices. A program could be built along the lines of postage meters, where the devices are monitored and owned by regulated financial firms. The challenge is that the technology is outpacing these types of controls, as even stamps can be purchased and printed via Web sites and it is no longer necessary to have a postage meter.

The final reality may be that the move toward digital currency and e-money will require an entirely different control model. As the above indicates, continuing to cling to an outmoded process can result in more deterioration and migrating to a process that better fits emerging business realities. This will be very difficult, as the current process is the result of decades of progressive legislation. But like the Maginot Line, and despite the brilliance of its design, when it was built is not the question. The utility of the design, in the face of new technology, is the question. A system designed around cash and focused on teller-level interactions may be modifiable to fit this new reality. But, increasingly, it is looking like it may not.

Building Appropriate Controls into Online Payment Systems

When it comes to cyber payment systems, regulators have much more control. As with online casinos, they can effectively ban participation by using regulations to ban financial transfers to these systems. The specific aspects that need regulatory review include:

- How the confidentiality and privacy of the buyers will be observed, because customers, if only from a consumer protection standpoint, need to know what the appropriate guidance is so that they can determine if a provider is in compliance.
- Local regulatory enforcement is necessary to limit access to the data obtained in the cyber payment system; this prevents embarrassing surveillance and invasion of privacy.

- The stability of the cyber payment system, including its ability to be regulated by another if subsequently acquired.
- Regulatory recognition for these systems will work to bring them within the regulatory environment. Without a path to inclusion, these systems will define themselves outside of the regulatory envelope.

As with online casinos, the prohibition approach is counterproductive and a compliance-based approach would have led to greater control and oversight opportunities.

Within the context of an online cyber payment program, properly designed regulation could ensure AML principles and effective international cooperation. Most cyber payment plans intend to be global operators, so their implementation of the guidelines should be global as well. If there is a commonality of the principles, it must include a convergence of mechanical and operational guidelines. These measures should be under the direction of anti-abuse rules. Standardization or at least compartmentalization of the products offered by the industry will occur as part of the natural path of global growth. The only question is whether the current regulatory programs can get organized enough to be partners in creating a regulated industry—or adversaries in a battle over jurisdiction.

Although the theme of government intervention is focused on enforcement and compliance, as an emerging area, governing bodies have a window to participate as much as possible to positively impact the cyber payment business model. To alleviate these concerns, the foundation should be the current structure of the bank secrecy laws, focusing on both protection of customer records and provision for enforcement of laws. In this way, rather than reacting to money laundering crimes, there may be more initial cooperation and thus effective control over the evaluation in cyber payments.

Global Coordination on Future Issues

Assuming that such agreement can be reached, the next step is to build an appropriate model for global coordination of law enforcement in regard to cyber laundering.

Applying existing policies would dictate that different classes of potential customers have different risk profiles. Since cyber laundering will immediately attract money launderers interested in abusing these processes, the delivery platforms should anticipate that these high-volume customers need to be controlled differently than the occasional user who transacts very low volumes of business. So, to begin, all cyber payment plans should implement a "know-your-customer" policy for any customers who transact more than $3,000 in a two-week period. This would not impact the rare user or the volume user, though it would set different levels of authentication for each. This kind of flexible program provides a reasonable line that complies with the intent of customer identification programs and can be readily applied on a global basis.

Data that can be used to help establish the customer identification includes various name and contact details, plus specific access date, including:

- ISP account information, including the IP address used when accessing the account
- Other accounts linked to the same ISPs and/or IP address
- If cyber payment allows a telephone service (such as customer service), use the following local telephone account maintained by the position

Weighing Access vs. Privacy

A more aggressive AML tactic would be a client-side security device to confirm customer identification. Use of security key dongles is well established. Such security keys could authenticate the end-client and help log the ISP and cyber payment system connection. This does not limit the cyber payment business base but it may be crucial for technologies that more effectively reduce the incidents of illegal money laundering. Such a connection would reduce the money launderer's ability to hide behind a proxy and the anonymous use of false information. An ISP that is willing to provide a better protected cyber payment plan will need to maintain user identity information with the appropriate registration and maintain a log that shows the flow of data associated with an IP address. These logs, within a certain time span, can provide this data to the appropriate regulators in the event of suspicious activity.

One of the biggest problems of cyber laundering is how to avoid misuse of card data. While smart cards are much more difficult to clone than traditional credit and debit cards, any technology can be replicated. So anti-theft provisions with these technologies should also be incorporated into AML efforts. Without proper controls, stored value cards, or even smart cards can be abused. One control is the use of biometric identifiers, even though this may be difficult to implement with the anticipated temporary nature of these cards.

Recoveries from money laundering schemes involving digital currencies face additional challenges unless adequate steps are taken to document users. Many of the early electronic currencies, including those backed by digital gold and the like, required only an e-mail address. Since the online payment processing companies accepted anonymous e-mail addresses, this effectively meant that they had no idea who their customers were. Because of this situation, fully developed with the bankruptcy of DigiCash, the anonymous digital currency concept has some clear regulatory challenges to successful implementation. However, it is still a legitimate possibility given the right implementation of the guidelines and under proper regulatory enforcement.

Electronic cash should not be lost as digital money. Some form of a paper trail is required. At some point in the process, real funds have to be transmitted to the specific digital currency entity, no matter if it is an electronic currency, a currency substitute, or some variation of the two. Though this may not be acceptable to the market for those services, it can provide a workable solution if the bank issuing the currency is related to the bank offering the digital cash. Thus, if the money is used for the illegal purchase, then the bank can find the origin of the money. In addition, if the deposit structure maintains appropriate records, then the documentation will exist to identify depositors. If the underlying concept is to provide true anonymity by shifting the customer to an electronic currency, then the source of that deposit and the identity of the customer will remain anonymous, too. But it is unlikely that global AML authorities will agree to work with an entity that provides this level of anonymizing services. By definition, this would constitute a shell bank and be prohibited from establishing accounts unless it could provide full details about its customers.

Compliance Issues

Having an online banking program to validate compliance with the global AML efforts to combat cyber laundering would meet the needs for due diligence. This can be performed with government auditors responding to money laundering or terror financing allegations, or law enforcement officials responding to criminal conduct. The use of automated testing eliminates the possibility of bias or corruption by presenting all accounts that meet the given characteristics. These technologies are common in fraud cases and are regularly used on technology related audits and compliance reviews. For example, if indicators point to an account that was opened with $7,000 and then received additional deposits ranging from $1,000 to $3,000, then the system can readily identify not only the accounts linked to those transactions but any other accounts that share those characteristics—even accounts that share those same (or similar) ratio characteristics. Use of automated technologies in the AML process can more effectively mine data for correlative properties than human beings.

Any effective AML system must be global. This is especially true with cyber laundering because the involved party can conceivably be located anywhere and, via the Internet, function everywhere. So if a serious effort to impact both active and potential cyber laundering is to be enacted, it will have to have a global commitment. The traditional approach would call for the creation of a centralized database of bad actors and implement a compliance protocol, including name checking and some high-level customer identity verification program, and, last, create a global monitor for cyber currency entities. While these are valid views, they miss the driving impact of technology. As these entities are created further from traditional financial institution space, they have less need to comply with banking regulations. This next generation of entities will provide bank-like services from a technology platform, not a banking platform. They will appeal to people who resent authority for philosophical reasons or for reasons of criminal conscience. Either way, a single country, or even group of countries, cannot impose standards. These standards will have to be mutually developed while these technologies are emerging. Otherwise, the opportunity will be missed.

Putting Recovery Plans into Action

The first challenge is to identify and prioritize the desired objectives. Without a clear understanding from senior leadership, the AML team may differ on these objectives, wasting valuable effort clashing with each other and finally going out in several different directions.

For many people, the first reaction to abuse of trust is often anger, and rightfully so. This is not only an attack on the organization; it is a betrayal by trusted insiders. Despite this honest reaction, it is important to move past retribution and identify the important goals and prioritize them. For many companies these come in three primary categories:

1. Punishment objectives for the perpetrators
2. Recovery objectives for the company
3. Process improvement objectives to lessen the chance that the scheme could reoccur in the future

Punishment of the wrongdoers is a legitimate goal, but one that can be complicated in execution. It may involve filing a criminal complaint or dealing with the matter in civil court. It may also involve press and publicity as well as employee morale issues. These factors must be explored and balanced early in the process, optimally before the scheme is even identified to ensure that the punishment and recovery options are fully thought out and developed.

Criminal Prosecution

Criminal prosecution of wrongdoers is a mechanism that most companies pursue. By filing a criminal complaint with the appropriate law enforcement agency, the perpetrator is publicly branded and faces potential jail or probation. While some companies shy away from the resulting press, a criminal conviction or guilty plea can be a very strong factor in presenting a fidelity claim or litigating a civil lawsuit for damages.

If criminal prosecution is a corporate objective, the AML team needs to have a member familiar with criminal procedures to oversee it. Filing a criminal referral is required for financial institutions in most countries. This process involves informing the law enforcement agency as to the specific facts in your case and presenting them with the evidence that a crime has been committed. Unfortunately, white collar crime is not a high priority for many jurisdictions and action will require that the company assemble the necessary evidence in advance.

Once the criminal referral is made, the company changes from advocate to victim, and the decision making shifts to the prosecutor. From this point forward, the company has no control over the prosecution and sentencing. Therefore, it is essential that the initial case to law enforcement includes all relevant details of the scheme and a detailed presentation of the facts, the key players, key documents, and a list of relevant witnesses.

Civil Remedies

The elements necessary to prepare the civil case are less complicated and more commonly understood. Once the internal investigation has progressed to the point that the primary players are identified, civil litigation becomes an option. The civil process opens up discovery procedures that can give the company access to third-party records, depositions, formal "on the record" answers, and other tools to complete the documentation of the fraud.

In preparing the civil claims, local counsel will be invaluable in providing information about local rules and practices. In some jurisdictions, discovery is automatic; in others it is delayed. Also, it can be problematic to introduce new parties to the suit in some jurisdictions, potentially making it difficult to add parties later determined to be involved. Operations and company auditors should be actively involved with the legal department to ensure that the discovery tools are best used to fill in any holes in the document trail.

With the recovery elements being collectively managed, the company can proceed on a balanced front to accomplish its objectives. Weighing any one section over the others will have a predictable result on the outcome, and many companies cause themselves unnecessary difficulties by stressing either legal or audit and not including AML or security in the process.

Conclusion

One of the trickiest areas for the project team to handle is size and involvement. Organizational dynamics differ, and the team will require management support to be effective. At the same time, a camel is a horse built by committee (as the joke goes), and the smaller the team can be, the more effective and efficient it will be in managing the investigation.

An ideal project team would include the AML team members, as well as representatives from the operations, audit, and legal departments as appropriate. While confidentiality is important, make sure that all appropriate knowledge is included to make the project successful. Otherwise, much expertise and valuable lessons will be lost. In many organizations, several layers of management and control will want to be involved. This is usually not helpful, both in the drain on management time and the potential to fall into inefficient large group meetings.

One strategy that several companies have used successfully is for the legal department to provide a restricted management briefing to selected people so that they are kept in the loop, while leaving the project team small enough to respond to changing conditions.

The final key to success is managing the process like any other project: Assemble the right team, empower them to respond as the situation warrants, structure a clear and unambiguous reporting chain, and let them do their job. In the above case, the team divided the myriad tasks along these lines, enabling them to deal with the complicated issues, quickly identifying and implementing a successful recovery strategy.

CHAPTER 11

Conclusion

That money laundering is illegal has done nothing to curb its spread. The evolution of global standards is helping the financial world catch up with the trading world. Because of regional accords, such as the North American Free Trade Agreement (NAFTA), emerging markets, such as India and China, and especially the creation of the World Wide Web, the world is smaller and money laundering has now become an occupation, not just a footnote in the compliance manual. Estimates of the size and pace of money laundering vary, but all agree that the advent of new digital currencies will position the financial sector for a significant change in method and approach to controlling money laundering. Learning methods and technology have expanded through banks and other businesses, permitting regulators and law enforcement to reduce and prevent the laundering of illegal funds. Nevertheless, just around the corner, money laundering can adapt to leap past the established control processes as banking services via electronic networks and other technologies evolve.

Historically, combating money laundering has been a cat-and-mouse game. From required paper records to the dawn of the cashless era, and with the regulators increasing requirements steadily, money launderers respond with more inventive schemes and abuses of technology. With the Patriot

Act, the focus shifted from the prosecution of narcotics traffickers to the suppression of terror financing. Since both use the same mechanisms, this effectively meant finding ways to screen for much smaller sized transactions. Through technology and training and audit provisions, the steps required to stop money laundering at brick-and-mortar level of banking are picking up speed. However, monetary accommodation, circulation, and alternative technologies are resulting in laundering processes that produce world-class clean money faster than ever before.

Fully realizing the risks that a given organization can be involved in money laundering activities leads to the best possible solutions. The risks inherent in Internet banking services and cyber payment systems are not extensions or expansions—they are game changers. For decades, financial tools changed slowly, enabling the stratification of policies and the entrenchment of control perspectives. With little understanding of the extent of the differences that cyber payment firms bring to the financial marketplace, regulators are trying to force fit cyber laundering mitigation procedures based on decades of brick-and-mortar experience. The problem is that these entities exist everywhere, but not under any regulator's specific jurisdiction. Their customers are in all nations, but have recourse to the courts; and the entities providing these services are not only nonbanks, they are typically not even financial companies—they are programming entities. They often have a disdain for rule and historical habit, and they see nothing wrong with investing in an entirely new way of operating—and they intend to offer products that compete with traditional banking.

Although the conventional money laundering legislation has been passed in nearly every country in the world, the same cannot be said for its electronic variations. Solutions require legislative, procedural, and, most important, consensus agreements on the role, regulation, and risk inherent to the various type of entities used by money launderers. With a decent foundation, professionals can use existing tools, as well as new initiatives, to identify possible illegal activities. Cyber laundering should be controllable once the current procedures are appropriately adapted, reporting and identification procedures are resolved, and the potential for abuse through criminals, illegal acts, money laundering, and terror financing are all properly controlled. The cyber laundering principle, while differing in form, is intended to duplicate the current anti-money laundering posture with the added responsibility to effectively cover the cyber payment system environment.

Money laundering remains a persistent theme in the press and in regulator and law enforcement circles. It is that most frustrating of situations, where the constant exchange of attack and defense continues. No doubt, money laundering and terror financing are increasing. The world, however, is also shrinking. Regulators and law enforcement work closely, and on a global scale, to uncover the genuine facts and figures ascribed to misconduct. The Financial Action Task Force (FATF) has successfully established coordination, laws, regulations, and enforcement on a global basis. What remains is determining the impact of money laundering activities despite the improvements. Continued difficulties in resolving international money laundering continue, and governments and the private sector are looking for a comprehensive vision into the next generation of solutions—solutions that will encompass the legal issues, regulators, law enforcement, the evolving financial industry, and the public at large.

About the Author

Jonathan E. Turner has spent his career focusing on the prevention, detection, and resolution of financial fraud, money laundering, and computer crime cases. He is a cofounder of Wilson & Turner Incorporated, where he works with leading companies worldwide, and his efforts have led to numerous multimillion-dollar recoveries from fraud schemes. He has been retained to provide expert testimony regarding fraud methodologies on behalf of governmental, public, and private organizations before federal and bankruptcy courts in the United States as well as international venues.

Mr. Turner has written more than 45 articles and book chapters and is a much sought after speaker and commentator on fraud, money laundering, and related topics. He teaches undergraduate and graduate students at the University of North Carolina–Chapel Hill and the University of Memphis as an adjunct faculty member. He lectures around the globe regarding fraud, money laundering, and the investigation of fraud to law enforcement, accounting, investigative, and regulatory professionals.

Mr. Turner is an active member of the Association of Certified Fraud Examiners (ACFE), where he is a faculty member and Regent Emeritus. He was elected Chairman of the Board of Regents for 2010 and has held numerous other leadership positions. He has been a board member and held leadership positions with other professional and civic groups. He was educated at Tulane University (BA, International Relations) and the

University of Leicester (MSc, Security & Risk Management) and is a Certified Fraud Examiner (CFE), Certified International Investigator (CII), and licensed private investigator.

In addition to the ACFE, Mr. Turner is an active member of the American Bar Association, the American Society of Criminology, and many other professional groups. He serves on the editorial boards of *Fraud Magazine* and the *John Liner Review*, and he is an advisor to the audit committees of several not-for-profit organizations.

Index